THE GERMAN EMIGRATION TO AMERICA

1709-1740.

*PART III. OF A NARRATIVE AND CRITICAL HISTORY,
PREPARED AT THE REQUEST OF*

The Pennsylvania=German Society.

BY REV. HENRY EYSTER JACOBS, D.D., LL.D.,

NORTON PROFESSOR OF SYSTEMATIC THEOLOGY IN THE THEOLOGICAL SEMINARY
OF THE EVANGELICAL LUTHERAN CHURCH IN PHILADELPHIA; TRANSLATOR AND EDITOR OF THE "BOOK OF CONCORD," SCHMID'S
"DOCTRINAL THEOLOGY OF THE EV. LUTHERAN CHURCH," "ELEMENTS OF RELIGION,"
ETC., ETC.

LANCASTER, PA.
1898

Printing Statement:

Due to the very old age and scarcity of this book, many of the pages may be hard to read due to the blurring of the original text, possible missing pages, missing text, dark backgrounds and other issues beyond our control.

Because this is such an important and rare work, we believe it is best to reproduce this book regardless of its original condition.

Thank you for your understanding.

PREFATORY NOTE.

The great movement of thousands of Palatines, accompanied by some Swabians and other Germans to England in the spring and summer of 1709, was traced in a most exhaustive and satisfactory manner last year. They had been preceded, it will be remembered, by a small band under the Rev. Joshua Kocherthal, who, after some delay in England, had reached New York on the last day of 1709. It is our aim to take up the narrative at this point, and, after following the course of the immigrants to Pennsylvania, to give some account of succeeding emigrations, until the year 1740.

CHAPTER I.—THE EFFORT TO TURN GERMAN EMIGRATION TO SOUTH CAROLINA.

KOCHERTHAL, upon whose tombstone at West Camp, New York, may still be read the inscription that he was "the Joshua to the High Germans in America,"[1] had been pastor at Landau, the now flourishing town in Bavaria, that had suffered exceedingly from repeated invasions by the French. In the year 1704, after the invasion of 1703, he had visited England to inquire into the expediency of an emigration of his people to America. The information which he gathered he embodied in a brochure, the first edition of which was pub-

---

[1] "Wisse Wandersman | Unter diesem Steine ruht | nebst seiner Sibylla Charlotte | Ein rechter Wandersmann | Der Hoch-Teutschen in America | ihr Josua | Und derselben an Der ost und west seite | Der Hudson Rivier | rein lutherischer Prediger | Seine erste ankunft war mit L'd Lovelace | 1707/8 den 1. Januar | Seine sweite mit Col. Hunter | 1710 d. 14 Juny | Seine Englandische reise unterbrach | Seine Seelen Himmlische reise | an St. Johannis Tage 1719 | Begherstu mehr zu wissen | So unter Suche in Welanchthons vaterland | Wer war dex de Kocherthal | Wer Harschias | Wer Winchenbach | B. Berkenmayer S. Heurtein L Brevort | MDCCXLII."

Außführlich und Umständlicher Bericht
Von der berühmten Landschafft
CAROLINA,
In dem Engelländischen America gelegen.

An Tag gegeben
Von

Kocherthalern.

Zweyter Druck.

Franckfurt am Mayn,
Zu finden bey Georg Heinrich Oehrling,
Anno 1709.

Pamphlet circulated by Kocherthal advising emigrants to go to Carolina.

lished in 1706, and the second edition at Frankfort on the Main in 1709. The title of this little volume, intended to advocate the claims of South Carolina in preference to those of Pennsylvania as the goal of German Emigration is: "Full and Circumstantial Report concerning the Renowned District of Carolina in English America."

Under what influence he had reached his conclusions he does not state. But the comparatively weak stream of immigrants that flowed to Pennsylvania in the first decade of the Eighteenth Century, in response to the many appeals, indicates a dissatisfaction and distrust, that suggested inquiries into the availability of other parts of America for German colonists. His argument in favor of choosing Carolina for the settlement, was preceded by ten chapters, concerning the land in general, the government, the fertility of the soil, the climate, the security, the voyage, etc. While the ordinary assignment of land was fifty acres to every head of a family, Mr. Kocherthal states that he has been promised one hundred and fifty, or even two hundred acres to each, in case the number of immigrants be large. The terms provide that the land shall be free for the first three years, and that, afterwards, the nominal rent shall be a penny per acre annually. With its glowing description of the fertility of the soil in wheat, rye, oats, barley and Indian corn, and its adaptation to the cultivation of the vine and tobacco, of olives and cotton; with the opportunities portrayed for the manufacture of silk by its facilities for the raising of mulberry trees; with an account of forests, full of valuable timber, and the vision of mines, rich in iron and lead; with a remarkable statement concerning the salubrity of the climate, where the temperature of the winter was no more rigorous than April or October in the Palatinate, and the summer, while warmer, was tempered by almost constant cool breezes, where the days were two hours shorter in summer, and two hours longer in winter than in Germany; and with assurances of the friendship of the Indians, and the freedom offered by the Government, we can readily understand how the book spread among oppressed and impoverished people dissatisfaction with their homes, and enkindled the desire to cross the ocean to the new land of promise.

Pennsylvania, it was conceded, had certain advantages. German settlements had already been founded, and the fruits of the soil were chiefly those to which Germans were accustomed. But these, it was maintained, were overbalanced by the eternal summer, and never failing pasturage, and less expensive homes and clothing for colonists, and shelter for the wintering of cattle. The voyage to Pennsylvania required an immediate outlay, while all the expense of the trip to Carolina could be defrayed by subsequent service in the colony.

To the credit of Kocherthal, be it said that he did not hide any of the dangers and difficulties in the way of removal to America. The peril of the long sea voyage and the many hardships to be faced after landing were faithfully narrated. His readers were warned against being influenced by the desire for riches, or for an easy life, or by the love of adventure, and mere curiosity. The opportunity was one only for those, for whom all other support had failed. His closing statement, that, in the year 1708, or at farthest, in the spring of 1709, he intended to set out for Carolina, with his family and a number of others, and his invitation, upon certain conditions, for additional recruits, carry us to the very source of the Palatinate movement to England as the portal to America.

So inaccessible is this volume to most investigators, that an extended synopsis is here given:

"CHAPTER I.—*Of the Country.*

"Boundaries of Carolina. Division into North and South Carolina. Advantages of the latter: Settled along the Ashley and Cooper rivers, with some Reformed Swiss along the Santee. Otherwise South Carolina is unsettled. Distance from nearest part of South Carolina to nearest part of Pennsylvania, 100 German miles. Route: From Germany to Holland; thence to England; thence southwest to 900 or 1000 German miles. Coast low; interior elevated, with some high mountains.

"CHAPTER II.—*Of the Government.*

"South Carolina was given by the King of England in 1663 to some noblemen, as a reward for fidelity, who have transmitted it by inheritance to present owners. Government consists of eight persons, of whom Lord Granville is President. A governor rules in their name. Religious freedom assured Reformed and Lutherans alike, and also to the Mennonites. Every head of a family can procure 50 acres, or, if he need them, 100 acres of land. As a special favor,

150 or even 200 acres were offered Kocherthal, in case a large number settle together. Any unsettled portion of Province may be chosen by settlers under this offer. No rent for first three years; afterwards, a penny an acre annually; but as another special favor, if a large number of settlers accompany him, the number of free years will be extended, possibly as high as seven. Tithes will be required for Church purposes. Removal to another province permissible at any time, upon payment of all debts, and due notice to the Government. Mechanics will be required to pay only a few pence of taxes annually. Hunting and fishing free, the only restriction being that of not trespassing on lands of other settlers, or coming too close to the Indians.

"CHAPTER III.—*Of the Fruitfulness of the Soil.*

"South Carolina is one of the most fruitful countries to be found. Far surpasses England and Germany. But districts vary in their productivity. Two crops of Indian corn may be raised in a season. No better rice is raised in any land. It is an extensive article of commerce. French settlers have been very successful in the cultivation of grapes. Tobacco rivals that of Virginia. Apples, pears, plums, quinces, etc., may be raised from seed, which settlers should bring with them. The mulberry tree offers opportunities for silk-culture. Much may be expected from the raising of cotton. Olives, citrons, figs, pomegranates flourish. Although iron and lead mines have been opened, yet as it requires a large amount of capital to work them, settlers should bring their iron tools with them. All sorts of domestic animals may be raised. Cattle need not be housed in winter, which in South Carolina has the temperature of April or October in Germany. Swine may be raised with scarcely any cost, since the forests abound in acorns. Rare opportunities for hunting, especially of swans, ducks, geese and other water fowls. A cow may be bought for an English pound. The cultivation of indigo and tea offers rich returns.

"CHAPTER IV.—*Of the Climate.*

"Occasionally, some snow or ice, early in the morning during winter, but it disappears by eight or nine o'clock. While the heat in summer is considerably greater than in Germany, yet at sunset a cool breeze tempers the atmosphere, and renders it more tolerable than in Virginia, notwithstanding the fact that the latter is farther north. The weather not uniform. Places and seasons differ. Generally the climate is very healthful. The Indians used frequently to attain the age of 100, but their age limit has been shortened, since they have learned from Europeans to be intemperate in eating and drinking. It requires some months for immigrants to be acclimated. Carolina unsurpassed in abundance of medicinal herbs.

"CHAPTER V.—*Of Peace and Security.*

"Not only entire peace, but, so far as man can foresee, no future wars, ever to be apprehended. The Indians all friendly, and, besides, ignorant of European modes of warfare. On the right, the other English settlements form a barrier and protection against all possible attacks, while, on the left, the Spaniards are so few, that they fear the English, rather than the latter them. Sand bars exclude enemies by sea. The scene of the naval war which England is carrying on with the French and Spaniards, is on the Caribbean Sea, 100 to 150 German miles from Carolina. Although there are some wolves in wild portions of the Province, they prey upon other animals that abound, and rarely attack men. Serpents are not more numerous than in Italy, Spain and other warm countries, and avoid the settlements.

"CHAPTER VI.—*Of Commerce.*

"Carolina has an extraordinary number of navigable rivers, rendering the transport of the fruits of the soil from the interior to other parts of the Province, the West Indies and Europe, most easy. Coins, with some slight difference, the same as with us. Final decision in all matters of litigation made according to English law and custom.

"CHAPTER VII.—*Of European Nations already in Carolina: Cities and Towns.*

"Thirty years since Carolina was first settled by English people. Three nationalities now represented, viz.: the English, the Dutch and the French. No Germans as yet, but most of the Dutch not only can understand, but even speak the German. Charleston, founded in 1680, on the Ashley and Cooper, and New London, on the Edisto, are chief places, and must be regarded as towns, rather than cities. All sorts of wares may be purchased in Charleston, yet, as the proportion of mechanics to the population is not as great as among us, prices are higher. Immigrants should bring with them as many implements as pos sible, especially those which are necessary for building. There are a number of schools. In Charleston, there is a Latin School, and in Virginia, a High School. The English, besides endeavoring to Christianize the Indians, are attempting to diffuse a literature among them.

" CHAPTER VIII.—*Of the Disadvantages of the Country.*

" The first and chief want of the country, is people, as the most of the land is unsettled and unpopulated. The length, expense and perils of the voyage. To Germans, it is a great disadvantage that none of their countrymen are there. All other objections are of small account, such as that in the beginning every thing is strange—the greater heat in summer, and the wolves and serpents, of which we have previously made mention.

" CHAPTER IX.—*Of the Voyage from England to Carolina.*

" In time of peace, ships go to Carolina or Virginia, almost every month, but in time of war, generally only in the spring and fall. Spring, the best time. If the wind be constantly favorable, and the voyage in other respects, prosperous, it may be completed in six or even five weeks, in rare cases, even in four; but otherwise it may consume a half a year. In peace, the fare is from five to six pounds sterling; but the cost of a convoy and other expenses, raise it to from seven to eight pounds for every adult. Special arrangements have to be made with the Captain for each half grown child. Persons too poor to pay

RICHARDI BLOME
Englisches
AMERICA,
oder
Kurtze doch deutliche
Beschreibung aller derer
jenigen Länder und Inseln
so der Cron Engeland in West-In-
dien ietziger Zeit zuständig und
unterthänig sind.
durch eine hochberühmte Feder
aus dem Englischen übersetzt
und mit Kupffern gezieret.

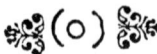

Leipzig /
Bey Johann Großens Wittbe und Erben.
Anno 1 6 9 7.

Blome's Description of the English possessions in the Western Hemisphere.

sometimes find proprietors willing to advance the funds, in return for which they serve the latter for some time in Carolina. The period of service, in time of peace, is from two to three years, but when the fare is higher, the time is necessarily longer. Those contemplating such payment, should write to England, and so arrange before starting. The author has endeavored in every way, to secure some other mode of providing for the passage. He has determined, in case a sufficient number to justify the attempt be enrolled, to apply to the Queen to transport them in the hope that they may be carried also on their way from Holland. He is unwilling to ask the favor unless a large number should respond to his proposition. How, in the midst of the other great expenses, and especially those of war, the Queen would be able to assume the responsibility the author does not know. He can make no promises; but can only hope that Divine Providence may open the way. Perils from storms, and, even with the convoy, of pirates must be faced; but ships thus guarded, have for some years been very rarely attacked.

"CHAPTER X.—*Of the Authority for what has been Mentioned.*

" A full report made by a French merchant, du Pre, to a friend in Amsterdam, under date of Maplica, February 17, 1703. Two trustworthy merchants in Holland, by the name of Bujotte, who lived long in Carolina, gave a circumstantial account of the land, in the presence of several other persons. A similar account was received from another London merchant. A number of statements from a sea captain, by the name of Cock. A merchant, by the name of Johnson, gave me a circumstantial account of the country. A clergyman gave much information he had received from the country itself. The Secretary of the Carolina Government also gave an account in the presence of the above mentioned clergyman. A German merchant resident in London, told me of what he had incidentally learned of the country in different places. Almost all the above information was given by the informants separately and independently. Information was also received from the Government. The literature utilized was a little book called Blome's *English America*, translated into the German, and published in Leipzig, 1697, the *Frankfort Relations* 1690, 1700, 1701, various letters in English newspapers concerning Carolina, the *Psychosophia* of Dr. Becher, in which he has written on the colonizing of the West Indies.

" APPENDIX.—*Of Pennsylvania*.

" After referring to Pastorius' *Pennsylvania* and Falckner's *Continuation of the Description of Pennsylvania*, both published at Nuremberg by Otto, Kocherthal, states that in his journey he had met a number of persons who had lived for years in Pennsylvania, and that, therefore, he would give some facts not published in the books mentioned. While Carolina has eternal summer, Pennsylvania has a very severe winter, and one that is not surpassed even in Germany. While in Carolina, the cattle can be kept in the fields all winter, in Pennsylvania they must be housed in barns. Grapes do not flourish as well in Pennsylvania as in Carolina, although the most diligent attempts have been made to cultivate them. In Caro-

lina, people will not suffer in the beginning even in very insignificant huts, whereas the cold winter compels buildings of a very substantial character to be immediately erected for cattle as well as men. The relative expense of clothing must also be remembered. The most desirable lands in Pennsylvania have already been taken, necessitating the purchase of ground from the first occupants, or the payment of much greater ground rent. An immigrant to Pennsylvania must have the money ready with which to prepay his passage, while for one going to Carolina, this is not necessary. Pennsylvania, however, has some advantages: It has German settlers who will aid their countrymen. Its fruits and grains more nearly correspond to those of Germany."

When, then, to this we add the record of lands donated to the Palatines by Queen Anne, along the Broad and Saluda, Congaree and Wateree rivers in South Carolina, near and around the present site of Columbia, the chain of evidence is completed. Although this district, a portion of which is still popularly known to the neighborhood, as "Dutch Fork," was settled by immigrants from southwestern Germany, they represent a late emigration. Some unknown cause intervened to thwart Kocherthal's plans.

CHAPTER II.—THE IMMEDIATE RESULTS OF KOCHERTHAL'S PAMPHLET.

REACHING England in the spring of 1708, Kocherthal's petition to the "Board of Trade" does not mention Carolina, but requests simply "to be sent to one of the plantations,[1] and even this secured a hearing only when three of the Lutheran clergymen of London appeared with him before the Board and pleaded his cause."

The part taken by the pastors of the three Lutheran churches in London deserves especial recognition. The most influential was Anton Wilhelm Boehme, pastor of the German Court Chapel of St. James, born 1643, a native of

---

[1] *Minutes of the Board of Trade*, April 26, 1708. "Mr. Joshua de Kocherthal with three Lutheran ministers (settled here) attending in relation to the ref. from Mr. Scy. Boyle, touching the settlement of the said K. and others in some of Her Majesty's Plantations in America."

Psalmodia Germanica:

OR, THE

GERMAN PSALMODY,

Translated from the

HIGH DUTCH.

TOGETHER

With their proper TUNES, and thorough BASS.

The THIRD EDITION, *Corrected and very much Enlarged.*

Non Vox, sed Votum, non Musica chordula sed Cor; non clamans, sed amans cantat in Aure Dei.

LONDON, Printed;

NEW-YORK, Re-printed, and sold by H. GAINE, at the *Bible & Crown*, in *Queen-Street*, 1756.

Facsimile of title page of *Psalmodia Germanica* (Third Edition); first edition, 1722. (Used by Muhlenberg in English services.)

Pyrmont, an alumnus of Halle, a pupil and frequent correspondent of Francke, and a man of devout spirit and distinguished literary gifts, whose influence was not only very great with Prince George of Denmark, the Queen's husband, whose spiritual adviser he was, but with the Queen herself. Boehme was the most important link between the German churches and the Church of England. It was by his intervention that the " Society for the Propagation of the Gospel in Foreign Parts" adopted and supported the Lutheran missions in East India, after the country passed from the Danish to the English government. His pen was active in the translation of Arndt's *True Christianity* and other standard German works, as well as the Reports of the Halle Mission House, into English, and in the publication in Germany of at least one important book concerning the English Church. Through his intercession Queen Anne endowed a "Free Table" in the Orphan House at Halle.

In the very serious project for a union between the Church of England and the Protestant Church of Germany, that was then the subject of negotiation, with the powerful support of the Queen, and that ceased only with her death, Boehme was probably one of the most important factors. From the arrival of the first emigrants in England, and through all their trials in America, until his death in 1722, they always had in him "a friend at court."[1] Associated with Boehme were George Andrew

---

[1] For biographical sketches of BOEHME, see JOCHER's *Gelehrten Lexicon;* STEPHEN's *Dictionary of National Biography;* Walch's *His-*

Ruperti and John Trebecco, both of whom frequently appeared before the Board of Trade on their behalf. Another official of St. James' Chapel who befriended them was John Christian Jacobi,[1] well-known as the translator of hymns still sung, of which "Holy Ghost Dispel our Sadness" may be cited as an example, and the editor of the *Psalmodia Germanica*, who was occasionally called in to act as interpreter.

After Pastor Kocherthal, with his band numbering originally twenty-six Calvinists and fifteen Lutherans[2]—increased afterwards by a few arrivals from England—had been entrusted to the care of Lord Lovelace, as Governor, and been sent, with generous provision, to New York, the influence of Kocherthal's pamphlet and example continued to work. When the "German Exodus to England" oc-

---

torische und Theologische Einleitung in die Religion—Streitigkeiten der Ev. Luth. Kirchen, Jena, 1733, Vol. V., pp. 111-399. Burckhardt's *Kirchen-Geschichte der Deutschen Gemeinden in London*, Tübingen, 1798, pp. 77-399. An interesting anecdote illustrating his character is told by Burckhardt, a later London Lutheran pastor. Boehme preached once with such earnestness against adultery that a nobleman in his audience interpreted the sermon as a personal attack, and challenged Boehme to a duel. The challenge was accepted. The pastor appeared on the field in his clerical robe, and with a Bible, instead of a pistol, in his hand. "I regret," he said, "that you were offended at my sermon against a most grievous sin. I can assure you that you were not in my mind. But here I am, armed with the sword of the Spirit, and if your conscience condemns you, I beseech you, for your salvation, to repent and reform your life. If you want to fire I am ready to lay down my life, if your soul only may be saved." List of his numerous publications in *Sammlung auser lesener Materien*, etc. Leipzig, 1733, pp. 38-47.

[1] Mr. Jacobi was Kocherthal's interpreter, Board of Trade Journals, June 14, 1708.

[2] Board of Trade, April 26, 1708.

Das verlangte / nicht erlangte Canaan bey den Lust-Gräbern;

Oder Ausführliche Beschreibung

Von der unglücklichen Reise derer jüngsthin aus Teutschland nach dem Engelländischen in America gelegenen

Carolina und Pensylvanien

wallenden Pilgrim / absonderlich dem einseitigen übelgegründeten

Kochenthalersschen Bericht

wohlbedächtig jutgegen gesetzt

In
I. Einem Beantwortungs-Schreiben etlicher diese Sach'angehenden Fragen; nebst einer Vorrede Moritz Wilhelm Höens.
II. Ermahnungs-Schreiben an die bereits dahin verreißte Teutsche / Anthon Wilhelm Böhmens.
III. Der Berg-Predigt Christi/ und Gebettern vor die noch dahin auf dem Weg begriffenen rc.

IV. Königl. Englischen deswegen nach Teutschland erlassenen Abmahnung.
V. Kurtzen Relation, jener dabey erlittenen Elendes und Schicksals.
VI. Noch einer andern Relation davon.
VII. Einem Stück der Warnungs-Predigt von Hn. Johann Tribeckö/ rc. den zurückreisenden in London gehalten.

Alles aus Liebe zur Wahrheit und patriotischem Wohlmeinen zusammen verfasset.

Franckfurt und Leipzig / M DCC XI.

Title page of Rev. Anton Wilhelm Boehme's answer to Kocherthal's "Carolina."

curred Mr. Boehme was not in that country, but the year after he writes that "14,000 persons had gone to England with the expectation of being transported to Carolina." Although Boehme's answer to Kocherthal's pamphlet did not appear until 1711, and is intended to discourage future movements, yet it throws much light upon the details of the emigration to New York.

The book really consists of a series of tracts, the titles of which all appear on its title-page, as follows: "The Canaan, sought for, but not found, by those who till the air; or a full description of the unhappy voyage of the Pilgrims who recently went from Germany to the English possessions in Carolina and Pennsylvania; especially directed against the one-sided, and unfounded report of Kocherthal. I. An Answer to Some Questions on this Subject, with an introduction by Moritz Wilhelm Hoen. II. Admonition to the Germans who have already journeyed thither, by Anton Wilhelm Boehme. III. The Sermon on the Mount, and Prayers, to be used by them, on the way. IV. Dissuasion Against Forsaking Germany by the English Crown. V. Short Account of their Misfortunes. VI. Another Account. VII. An Extract from the Sermon of John Trebecco, delivered in London to the emigrants. All bound together out of love for truth, and patriotic motives. Frankfort and Leipzig, 1711." Each of these parts is paged separately, showing that they were independent publications that were afterwards collected and bound under the one title.

The introduction, written in a Christian spirit, by Moritz Wilhelm Hoen, warns earnestly against the fever for emigration to America, and declares that neither in Europe, nor in America does a Christian have an abiding place. Every one embarking for America must be prepared for troubles, must be ready to die, must have at least one hundred Frankfort florins, and must support his family out of his own purse, for an entire year after his arrival. Pennsylvania or Carolina is the question that is then discussed. The advantages and disadvantages of each are carefully balanced against one another. The freedom in both provinces is shown to be equal. The excessive heat of South Carolina renders the raising of European corn difficult, but adapts it for grape culture. Pennsylvania, Boehme concludes, is better for the Lower Saxons, who are farmers, while Carolina has advantages for the Palatines and others, who are wine producers. The argument for emigration, urged from religious motives, claims consideration, and is answered by the sententious remarks: "Some tell us that they are seeking religious repose. To such I say, 'The sun that shines at Cologne, shines also at Paris.' Calm must be sought inwardly, not outwardly. Every new mode of life has its peculiar temptations." To those who advised emigration because they believed that God's judgments upon a sinful land were about to descend, and that a Zoar or a Pella must be sought for in America, the sober answer is made, that no Christian has the right to flee from the judgments that his own sins, as well as those of others, have called down; and that if God place us in the midst of corrupt times, it is our duty not to abandon our post, but to remain, and give our testimony and make our protest. To the excuse that Germany was pervaded by sectarianism, Boehme answers that Pennsylvania has far more sects than Germany. It is, "a *colluvies* or *Mischmass* of sects, parties and opinions."

Although Pastor Kocherthal never saw the Carolina, which he had portrayed as a land of milk and honey, some of those who followed him the next year to England did. The Swiss baron, Christopher de Graffenried and Franz Louis Michel from Berne, reached England that season, with a colony of their countrymen, destined for the district between the Cape Fear and Neuse rivers in North Carolina. They were strengthened by a reinforcement of six hundred and fifty Palatines in two vessels. Most liberal provision was made for giving them an excellent start in their new home. Each family was allowed two hundred and fifty acres of land, without remuneration for five years; and afterwards upon a rental of two pence per acre, while, upon similar easy terms, they were supplied with agricultural implements, buildings, cattle, clothing and other necessaries. The full text of Graffenried's agreement is as follows:

DE GRAFFENDRIED'S CONTRACT.[1]

"Articles of Agreement, indented and made, published and agreed upon, this tenth day of October, Anno Domino one thousand seven hundred and nine, and in the eighth year of the reign of our sovereign, lady Anne, by the grace of God queen of Great Britain, France and Ireland, defender of the faith, between Christopher de Graffenrid of London esquire and Lewis Mitchell of the same place, of the one part, and sir John Philips bart. sir Alexander Cairnes bart. sir Theodore Janson knt. White Kennet D.D. and dean of Peterborough, John Chamberlain esquire, Frederick Slore doctor of physic, and Mr. Micajah Perry merchant, seven of the commissioners and trus-

---
[1] Williamson's History of North Carolina, I., 275-281.

tees nominated and appointed by her majesty's late gracious letters patent, under the great seal of Great Britain, for the collecting, receiving, and disposing of the money to be collected for the subsistence and settlement of the poor Palatines lately arrived in Great Britain, on the other part.

"Whereas the above named Christopher de Graffenrid and Lewis Mitchell have purchased to themselves and their heirs in fee, and are entitled to a large tract of land in that part of her majesty's dominions in America called North Carolina, which now lies waste and uncultivated for want of inhabitants; and they the said Christopher de Graffenrid and Lewis Mitchell have applied themselves to the commissioners appointed by the letters patent above mentioned for the subsistence and settlement of the poor depressed Palatines, that some number of the said poor Palatines may be disposed of and settled in the said tract in North Carolina aforesaid, as well for the benefit of the said Christopher de Graffenrid and Lewis Mitchell as for the relief and support of the poor Palatines.

"And whereas the said commissioners have thought fit to dispose of for this purpose six hundred persons of the said Palatines, which may be ninety-two families more or less, and have laid out and disposed of to each of the said six hundred poor Palatines the sum of twenty shillings in clothes, and have likewise paid and secured to be paid to the said Christopher de Graffenrid and Lewis Mitchell the sum of five pounds ten shillings lawful money of Great Britain for each of the said six hundred persons, in consideration of and for their transportation into North Carolina aforesaid, and for their comfortable settlement there.

"It is constituted, concluded and agreed, by and with the said parties to those psents in manner following :

"Inprimis that the said Christopher de Graffenrid and Lewis Mitchell, for the consideration aforesaid, at their own proper costs and charges, shall within the year next after the date hereof, embark or cause to be embarked on ships board, in and upon two several ships, six hundred of such of the said poor Palatines as shall be directed by the said commissioners, which together may in all make up ninety-two families more or less, and cause the said persons to be directly transported to North Carolina aforesaid, providing them with food and other necessaries during their voyage thither.

"Item, that upon the arrival of the said six hundred poor Palatines in North Carolina aforesaid, the said Christopher de Graffenrid and Lewis Mitchell shall, within three months next after their arrival there, survey and set out or cause to be surveyed and set out, by metes and bounds, so much of the said tract of land above mentioned as shall amount to two hundred and fifty acres for each family of the said six hundred poor Palatines, be they ninety-two families, more or less; and that the said several two hundred and fifty acres for each family be as contiguous as may be for the mutual love and assistance of the said poor Palatines one to another, as well with respect to their exercise of their religion as the management of their temporal affairs.

"And for avoiding disputes and contentions among the said Palatines in the division of the said several two hundred and fifty acres of land, it is agreed that the said land, when so set by two hundred and fifty acres to a family, be divided to each family by lot.

"Item, that the said Christopher de Graffenrid and Lewis Mitchell, their heirs, executors and administrators, within three months rest after the arrival of the said poor Palatines in North Carolina aforesaid, shall give and dispose of unto the said poor Palatines, and to each family by lot, two hundred and fifty acres of the tract of land above mentioned, and by good assurances in law grant and convey the said several two hundred and fifty acres to the first and chief person or persons of each family, their heirs and assigns forever, to be held the first five years thereafter, without any acknowledgment for the same, and rendering and paying unto the said Christopher de Graffenrid and Lewis Mitchell, their heirs, executors and administrators, for every acre the sum of two pence, lawful money of that country yearly and every year after the said term of five years.

"Item, that for and during one whole year after the arrival of the said poor Palatines in North Carolina aforesaid, the said Christopher de Graffenrid and Lewis Mitchell shall provide or cause to be provided for, and deliver to the said poor Palatines sufficient quantities of grain and provision and other things for the comfortable support of life; but it is agreed, that the said poor Palatines respectively repay and satisfy the said Christopher de Graffenrid and Lewis Mitchell, their heirs, executors and administrators, for the full value of what they shall respectively receive on the amount at the end of the first year then next after.

"Item, that the said Christopher de Graffenrid and Lewis Mitchell, at their own proper costs and charges, within four months after their arrival there, shall provide for the said Palatines and give and deliver or cause to be given and delivered to them, for their use and improvement, two cows and two calves, five sows with their several young, two ewe sheep and two lambs, with a male of each kind, who may be able to propagate; that at the expiration of seven years thereafter each family shall return to the said Christopher de Graffenrid and Lewis Mitchell, their heirs or executors, the value of the said cattle so delivered to them, with a moiety of the stock then remaining in their hands, at the expiration of the said seven years.

"Item, that immediately after the division of the said two hundred and fifty acres among the families of the said Palatines, the said Christopher de Graffenrid and Lewis Mitchell shall give and dispose of gratis to each of the said Palatines a sufficient number of tools and implements for felling of wood and building of houses, etc.

"And lastly, it is covenanted, constituted and agreed, by and between all parties to these presents, that these articles shall be taken and construed in the most favorable sense for the ease, comfort and advantage of the said poor Palatines intending to settle in the country or province of North Carolina; that the said poor Palatines doing and performing what is intended by these presents to be done on their parts, shall have and enjoy the benefits and advantages hereof without any further or other demand of and from the said Christopher de Graffenrid and Lewis Mitchell, their heirs, executors and administrators, or any of them; and that in case of difficulty it shall be referred to the governor of the country or province of

North Carolina, for the time being, whose order and directions, not contrary to the intentions of these presents, shall be binding upon the said Christopher de Graffenrid and Lewis Mitchell, his heirs, executors and administrators, as to the said poor Palatines.

"Witness whereof the said parties to these presents have interchangeably set their hands and seals the day above written.

"JOHN PHILIPS (L.S.)
"ALEXR. CAIRNES (L.S.)
"WHITE KENNET (L.S.)
"JOHN CHAMBERLAIN (L.S.)
"FREDERICK SLORE (L.S.)
"MICAJAH PERRY (L.S.)"

"Sealed and delivered by the within named, sir John Philips, Alexander Cairnes, White Kennet, John Chamberlain, Frederick Slore, Micajah Perry, having two six penny stamps.

"In presence of us
"WILLIAM TAYLOR,
"JAMES DE PRATT.

"We, the within named Christopher de Graffenrid and Lewis Mitchell, for ourselves, or heirs, executors and administrators, do hereby covenant and agree to and with the commissioners and trustees within written, for and upon the like consideration mentioned, to take and receive fifty other persons in families of the poor Palatines, to be disposed of in like manner as the SIX hundred Palatines within specified, and to have and receive the like grants, privileges, benefits and advantages as the said six hundred Palatines have, may or ought to have, in every article and clause within written, and as if the said fifty Palatines had been comprised therein, or the said articles, clauses and agreements had been here again particularly repeated and recited on to them.

"Witness our hands and seals, this 21st day of October, A.D. 1709.

"CHRISTOPHER DE GRAFFENRID,
"LEWIS MITCHELL.

"Sealed and delivered this agreement,
 in the presence of
"WILLIAM TAYLOR,
"JAMES DE PRATT.

Reaching the junction of the Neuse and Trent rivers in December, 1709, the town founded was called by its founders New Berne, after the city in Switzerland whence their leaders came.

Upon this colony, there burst in September, 1711, without warning, a fearful massacre. The Tuscarora Indians, who had hitherto been friendly, were excited to war by the schemes of English adventurers plotting against the administration of Governor Hyde. John Lawson, the first historian of North Carolina, and the Surveyor General, who had boasted that the foundation of North Carolina had been laid without shedding a drop of blood, had accompanied the Baron up the Neuse river, when they were seized and condemned to death by the Indians. Lawson perished by a most cruel death, while the Baron saved his life by claiming to be the King of the Palatines, and asking his captors whether they dared to put a King to death. Before his liberation, in October, a treaty was concluded, with the stipulation that in case of war between the English and the

Indians, the Palatines would remain neutral, and that, without agreement with the Indians, no more land would be taken up.[1] Meanwhile, however, September 22d, in accordance with a plan to exterminate all settlers south of Albemarle Sound, the Indians entered the settlements simultaneously, in small parties of six or seven, and within three days slew over one hundred colonists. The provisions of the treaty preventing the Palatines from joining in the war against the Tuscaroras, that followed, alienated from them their neighbors, who were ignorant how, through their assumed neutrality, they were constantly receiving and transmitting valuable information to the English leaders. When tired of the project, with its grave responsibilities and dangers, De Graffenried sold the land of the colony which had been deeded to him, to Thomas Polloch, no attention was paid to the just claims of the Palatines. But the wrong was righted when they filed their petition stating the facts.

Before, however, such a recompense was made a portion of the colonists, in their discouragement, consisting of twelve families and fifty persons, embarked for the north, and were wrecked in April, 1714, on the Rappahanock river in Virginia. Here they were settled by Governor Spottswood on his plantation, known after them as Germanna, about twelve miles above Fredericksburg. Thither they were sent partly to work his iron furnace and partly to defend the frontier. He says that he "built a fort,

---

[1] See Graffenried's Memorandum of this Treaty, transmitted to Governor Hyde in Williamson's *North Carolina*, Appendix to Vol. I., p. 287.

THE PENNSYLVANIA-GERMAN SOCIETY.

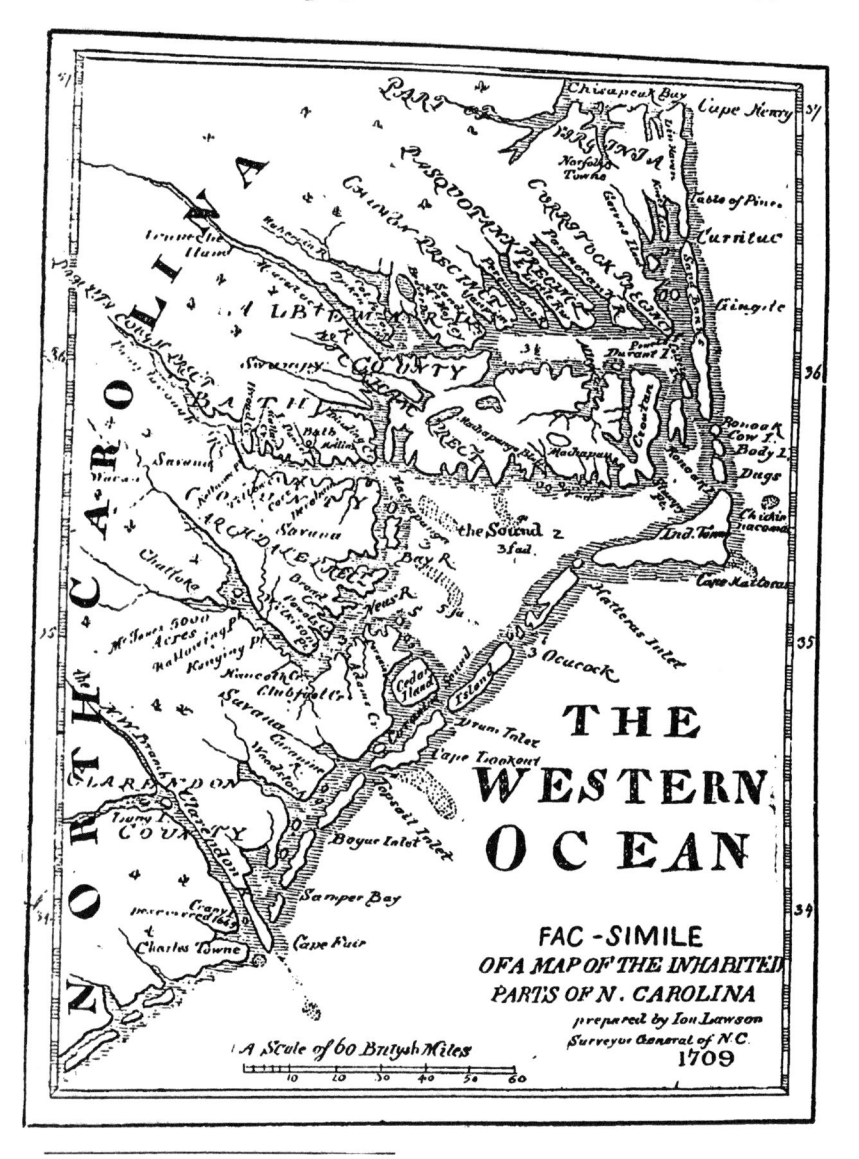

Map of North Carolina drawn by the murdered surveyor general.

and armed it with two pieces of cannon," to " awe the struggling parties of Northern Indians, and be a *good barrier for all that part of the country*." By successive divisions of counties, as well as by the removal of the site ten miles farther up the river, this colony was successively in Spottsylvania, Orange, Culpeper and Madison counties. Their first home was described by Col. Byrd in 1733, as " a baker's dozen of ruinous tenements," with a chapel that had been burned by " some pious people, with the intent to get another built nearer their own homes."[1] In this colony of Swiss and Palatines was the venerable Reformed clergyman, Rev. Henry Hoeger, then seventy-five years old. An important

The Tobacco Plant.

addition was made to their number by twenty families consisting of eighty persons from the Palatinate and Alsace, who, on their way to Pennsylvania, were detained for a long time in England by the arrest of the captain of their ship for debt—an incident which caused the failure of their provisions before they reached this side of the ocean, and

---

[1] *Official Letters of Alex. Spottswood*, Lieutenant-Governor of Colony of Virginia, Richmond, 1882.

Hebron Ev. Lutheran Church, Madison County, Virginia; built A.D., 1740.

the loss of many comrades from starvation. Wrecked at last in 1717 on the Virginia coast, they were sold by their captain as slaves to Governor Spottswood, who sent them to join their countrymen at Spottsylvania. This colony gave to Virginia the ancestors of the late Governor Kemper. Such was the lot of those who had been diverted, by Kocherthal's appeal, from Pennsylvania to Carolina.[1]

---
[1] *A Journey to the Land of Eden*, by *William Byrd* (1733). Reprinted, Richmond, Va , 1866, I., 59.

Arms of the Holy Roman Empire.

CHAPTER III.—THE PALATINATE EMIGRATION TO NEW YORK.

Arms of the Chur-Pfaltz.

FAR more important than these southern colonies was the large emigration in 1709 to New York. Kocherthal, with his fifty-three companions, had reached New York on the last day of the year, 1708, and founded Newburg on the Hudson, called after Neuburg in the Palatinate, where more than twenty-one hundred acres were assigned them, a glebe of five hundred acres being the share of Kocherthal himself. The death of Lord Lovelace, in May, 1709, who, from his own resources, had advanced four to five hundred pounds for their support, induced Kocherthal to sail for England during that summer, in order to secure aid for his sorely pressed people. On his arrival, he was kindly heard, and his petitions granted. The ultimate decision to send a thousand of his countrymen upon the same course that he had taken, was probably due in large measure to his presence. As early as May 18th, Pastors Trebecco and Ruperti, in the absence of Boehme, informed the Board of Trade, that many of the people had expressed the desire to be sent after their friends to New York. But it was long

Lord Lovelace.

before their destination was fixed. The Board inclined towards sending them to Jamaica, to recruit the small contingent of twenty-five hundred white settlers, among the forty thousand negroes on the island; and many days were spent in arranging the details for their transportation.

Bids for provisions for the use of one thousand persons on the voyage were invited, and the plan for their settlement was adopted and signed, when it was suddenly abandoned for another.

For years, the Board of Trade had been exercised with schemes for the gathering of naval supplies from the colonies. Reports in person and in writing were frequently heard from an officer especially appointed for this duty, John Bridger, who examined into the availability for this purpose, of the forests, from New England to Carolina. It was at last concluded that the pine forests of New York could be made to furnish ample tar and pitch; and that for their manufacture, the Palatines could be profitably used. With this end in view, Col. Robert Hunter was selected to succeed Lord Lovelace.

Seal and Autograph of Gen. Hunter.

Hunter wielded both pen and sword. The intimate friend of Swift and Addison and Steele, he is credited with the authorship of a classical essay on "*Enthusiasm*" once ascribed to Swift. As a Major he had been wounded at Blenheim. Appointed Lieutenant-Governor of Virginia, he had sailed May 20, 1707, but had been captured by privateers and carried to France, where, during the preceding winter, without suffering many serious restraints, he had been detained as a prisoner of war. Under date of November 30, 1709, Hunter presented an elaborate plan for the settlement of three thousand Palatines in New York, in reply to suggestions of the Board two months earlier, which, after several days' discussion, was adopted. An allowance of between three and four pounds a head was to be made for transportation, and of forty shillings a head for agricultural implements, while the land was to be allotted upon the same terms as to Kocherthal and his colonists of the preceding year. Under penalty of the forfeiture of their patents, they were forbidden to manufacture woolen goods. Before embarking they were to be naturalized as subjects of Great Britain. Mr. Boehme, in a postscript to his answer to Kocherthal, has given the regulations concerning naturalization. The person to be naturalized must appear in England, must be furnished with a certificate from a Protestant clergyman, endorsed by several other witnesses, that he has received the Lord's Supper in a Protestant church, and must take the oath of allegiance to the Queen of England. The Board had suggested that the Palatines would be "a good barrier between Her Majesty's subjects and the French and their Indians," and to this end the settlement must be either along the Hudson or the Mohawk, where there would also be peculiar facilities for the manufacture of turpentine, tar, pitch and rosin. Forty acres, subject after seven

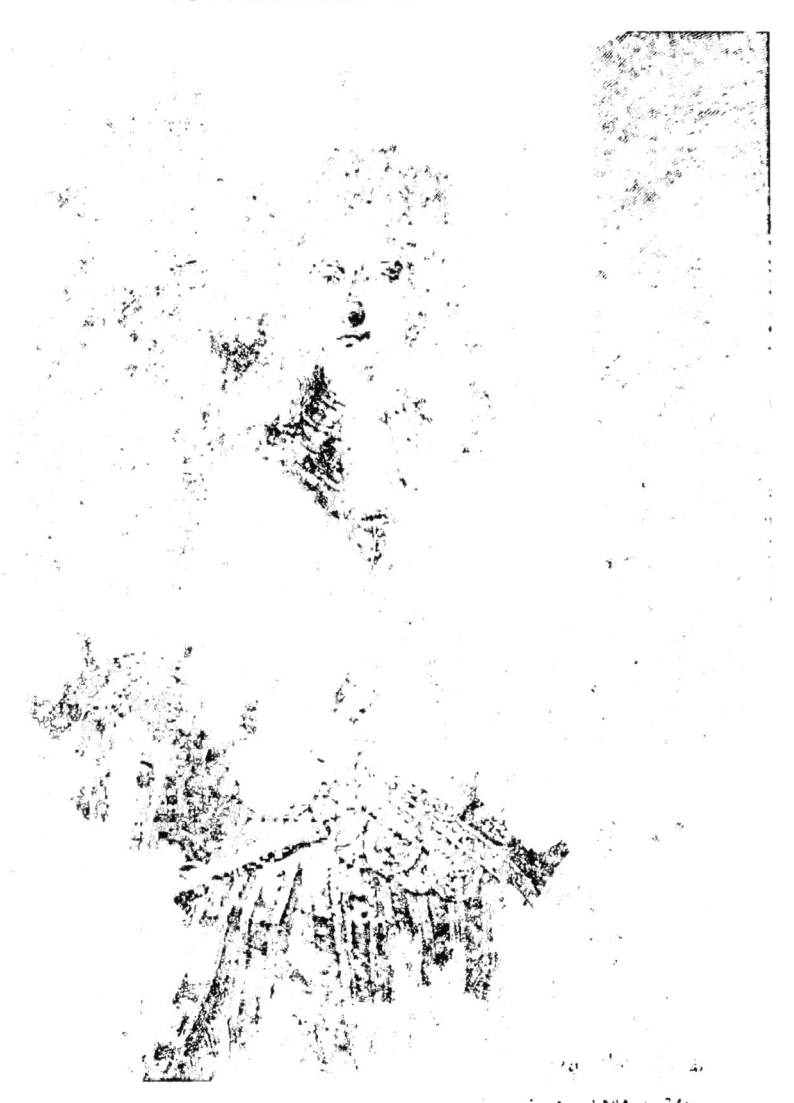

THE PENNSYLVANIA GERMAN SOCIETY

years to a quit rent, were to be given each family " after they shall have repaid, by the produce of their labor, the charges the public shall be at, in settling and subsisting them there." Because of their poverty provision is made also for their support until they shall be able to provide for themselves, which would not be at the soonest for less than a year. The calculation, according to which the Board demonstrated that the scheme would afford the Government ample remuneration for every penny expended, read like many promising projects of more recent speculators. One man, by his own labor, they said, could annually produce six tons of these stores. Where, however, a number were associated, the productibility of each man was doubled. Six hundred men, therefore, might be reasonably expected to make seven thousand tons a year. But their eloquence with the pencil reached its climax in the suggestion that if more would be produced by the Palatines than could be consumed in Great Britain, a profitable trade in these commodities with Spain and Portugal would be assured! There was only one difficulty in the way: The Palatines were as yet absolutely innocent of any knowledge of this art whereby they were to enrich the British Government! Instructors in the process were, therefore, a necessity; and yet it was not certain that such could be procured. Six hundred tents and the same num ber of firearms, with bayonets, are mentioned as important items to be included in the supplies.

By December 5th, the Board has decided that the Palatines must be settled in New York, "so as to give additional strength and security to that Province, not only with regard to the French of Canada, but against any insurrection of the scattered nations of Indians in these parts, and, in process of time, by intermarrying with the neighboring Indians (as the French do), they may be capable of rendering very great service to Her Majesty's subjects there; and not only very much promote the Fur Trade, but, likewise, the increase of Naval Stores." From Hunter's report it appears that not only the settlements on the Piscataqua River, or New Hampshire, but that even those on the Kennebec in Maine, were under discussion as suitable homes.

Meanwhile an instrument revised by Attorney-General Montague, entitled "*Covenant for the Palatines' Residence and Employment in New York*," was subscribed by each of the responsible emigrants after it had first been translated and read to them in German. To this document, and to the fact that it had been understood when signed, Governor Hunter appealed when, in 1720, he appeared in the presence of the elder Weiser before the Board of Trade, to answer the charge of having wronged the Palatines, and to meet their claim for possessions in the Schoharie district. It certainly binds the Palatines very tightly, and, although they heard it in their own language, their anticipations of the ease with which its conditions could be fulfilled when they would reach America, were such that they probably did not consider all that was involved.

Covenant for the Palatines' Residence and Employment in New York.[1]

"Whereas, we the underwritten persons, natives of the Lower Palatinate of the Rhine, have been subsisted, maintained and supported ever since our arrival in this kingdom by the great and Christian charity of Her Majesty, the Queen, and of many of her good subjects; and, whereas Her Majesty has been graciously pleased to order and advance a loan for us, and on our behalf of several very considerable sums towards the transporting, maintaining and settling of us and our respective families in Her Majesty's Province of New York in America, and towards the employing of us upon lands, for that intent and purpose to be allotted to us, in the production and manufacture of all manner of naval stores, to the evident benefit and advantage of us, and our respective families, and whereas Her Majesty has been likewise graciously pleased to give Her royal orders to the Hon. Col. Robert Hunter, who has now Her Majesty's commission to be Captain General and Governor in Chief of the said Province, and to all Governors of the said Province for the time being, that as soon as we shall have made good and repaid to Her Majesty, Her heirs or successors, out of the produce of our labors in the manufactures we are to be employed in, the full sum or sums of money in which we already are or shall become, indebted to Her Majesty, by the produce of our labor in all manner of naval stores on the lands to that end to be allotted to us, that then he, the said Col. Robert Hunter, or the Governor or Governors of the said

---
[1] *Documents pertaining to Colonial History of New York*, V., 121 sqq.

Province for the time being shall give and grant to us and our heirs forever, to our own use and benefit, the said lands so allotted as aforesaid, to the proportion or amount of forty acres to each person, free from all taxes, quit rents or other manner of services for seven years, from the date of such grant, and afterwards subjected only to such reservations as are accustomed and in use in that Her Majesty's said Province.

"Now KNOW ALL MEN by these Presents, that we, the said underwritten persons, in a grateful sense, just regard and due consideration of the premises, do hereby severally for ourselves, our heirs, executors and administrators, covenant, promise and grant to and with the Queen's most excellent Majesty, Her heirs and successors, that we with our respective families will settle ourselves in such place or places as shall be allotted to us in the Province of New York on the Continent of America, and abide and continue resident upon the lands so to be allotted to us as aforesaid, in such bodies or societies as shall be thought useful or necessary either for carrying on the manufacture of things proper for naval stores or for the defence of us and the rest of Her Majesty's subjects against the French or any other of Her Majesty's enemies, and that we will not, upon any account, or any manner of pretext, quit or desert the said Province, without leave from the Governor of the said Province first had and obtained for so doing, but that we will, to our utmost power, employ and occupy ourselves and our respective families in the producing and manufacturing of all manner of naval stores upon the lands so to be allotted us, or on such other lands as shall be thought more proper for that purpose, and not concern ourselves in working up or making things belonging to the woolen manufacture, but behave ourselves in all things as becomes dutiful and loyal subjects, and grateful and faithful servants to Her Majesty, her heirs and successors, paying all due obedience to the said Hon. Col. Robert Hunter or to the Governor or Governors of the said Province for the time being, and to all magistrates and other officers who shall from time to time be legally appointed and set over us; and towards repayment of Her Majesty, her heirs and successors, all such sums of money, as she or they shall at any time disburse for our support and maintenance, till we can reap the benefit of the produce of our labors, we shall permit all naval stores by us manufactured to be put into Her Majesty's storehouses which shall be for this purpose provided, under the care of a commissary, who is to keep a faithful account of the goods which shall be so delivered, and we shall allow out of the neat produce thereof so much to be paid Her Majesty, her heirs and successors, as upon a fair account shall appear to have been disbursed for subsistence of us, or providing necessaries for our families. In witness, etc."

The precise date of the sailing from England of the colonists is in doubt. Conrad Weiser says: "About Christmas Day, we embarked." A contemporary German account says that they were on the sea from Christmas to Easter. Henry Bendysh, who had the contract to transport them, agreed that January 2d should be the date for their sailing. But the Queen had not actually signed the instructions to Hunter, until January 26th. Pastor Trebecco's sermon before the embarkation was preached on

January 20th. As was frequently the case, there may have been considerable delay at Portsmouth after the embarkation, and the vessels may have gradually received their passengers, so that the discrepancy of a month may be readily explained.

A like diversity occurs with respect to the number of the emigrants. Conrad Weiser's figure is four thousand,

Savoy Palace and Chapel.

which harmonizes with the statement of his father and Scheff to the Board of Trade in 1720. Bendysh contracted to carry in ten ships about three thousand three hundred. General Nicholson testified in 1720 that the number was about three thousand two hundred. A contemporary German account fixes it as three thousand and eighty-six; and all other statements we have noted give the estimate of three thousand.

With the emigrants, Pastor Kocherthal sailed on his return. A Reformed student of theology, John Frederick Hager, whose name is almost that of the Virginia Reformed pastor, received Episcopal ordination in England, and sailed in this expedition, as a missionary of the Society for the Propagation of the Gospel in Foreign Parts. A very important member of the party was John Conrad Weiser, Sr., a widower accompanied by eight of his children, one of whom, a boy then twelve years old, was to become one of the most prominent factors in the history of colonial Pennsylvania, and the ancestor of Governor J. A. Schultz and of the first Speaker of the House of Representatives of the United States, and his brother, Major General Peter Muhlenberg. With them also were the great grandfather of William C. Bouck, Governor of the State of New York, from 1843 to 1845, and the ancestor of the Revolutionary hero, General Herkheimer.

No artist has painted the embarkation of the Palatines on those ten vessels; and, yet, would not the theme be just as fruitful, and the subject as worthy, as that of the Pilgrims from Rotterdam? Many go forth to meet the trials of the new world, as veterans, who, by the desolations of war that had raged around them, from their earliest years, in their fatherland, have been well prepared for the post they are to fill, as a wall of protection to the English settlers against the Indians. In his hand, each of them carries a small prayer-book, provided, at the expense of Queen Anne, by the London German pastors. Opening the volume with much veneration, we find there the " Sermon on the Mount," and five prayers. One of these prayers that served to guide the devotion of many a distressed heart, amidst the terrors of the storm, the horrors of disease, the loss of loved ones, and the struggle with death, during the passage that followed, may be appropriately introduced :

"ETERNAL AND MERCIFUL GOD, Whose goodness is every morning new, and Whose faithfulness is great towards us, poor men, we praise, we worship, we adore Thee, and from our hearts thank Thee, this morning, that Thou hast so graciously protected us during the past night, not dealing with us after our sins, but showing towards us great patience and calling us to repentance, faith and eternal life. Of all such blessings for body and for soul, we are unworthy, O Lord. We confess before Thee our sins, that have been committed against Thee often and in many ways. Lord, be merciful unto us, and forgive our guilt according to Thy great mercy, for Christ's sake. Grant us also an earnest hatred of all sins, and renew us, by Thy Holy Spirit, that henceforth we may not be the servants of sin, but may walk in righteousness and holiness all the days of our lives, since Thou hast redeemed us through Christ, and bought us to be Thine own. Into thy faithful hands, then, O God, we commend our bodies and souls, and all that we have and are. Bless us especially with spiritual blessings, that acknowledging Thee more and more, we may love

THE PENNSYLVANIA-GERMAN SOCIETY.

and hold fast to Thy Word. Bless us also with temporal blessings, granting us health and peace and provision for our bodily needs, and caring for us and ours in all things. Unto Thee we commit all our ways. Rule and direct us all, as in Thy good counsel, Thou knowest it will be best for us."

The sermon preached by Mr. Trebecco in St. Catherine's church, London, January 20th, to many of the emigrants, vividly recalls the entire situation. No more

Trebecco Preaching to the Palatines in Savoy Chapel.

appropriate text could have been chosen. It was Deut. 8: 1-3: "All the commandments which I command you this day, shall ye observe and do, that ye may live and multiply and go in and possess the land which the Lord sware unto your fathers. And thou shalt remember all the way which the Lord thy God led thee these forty years in the wilderness, to humble thee, and to prove thee, to know what was in thy heart, whether thou wouldst keep his commandments or no. And he humbled thee and suffered thee to hunger, and fed thee with manna, which thou knewest not, neither did thy fathers know; that he might make thee know that man doth not live by bread only, but by every word that proceedeth out of the mouth of God doth man live." After explaining the passage, he continued:

"My beloved Palatines, you can easily see that I have selected this text carefully that you may remember it on your voyage, and learn to make a proper use of your condition as pilgrims. While in many particulars your pilgrimage is very unlike that of the children of Israel, there are still many others in which there is a great resemblance. The dissimilarity consists in the fact that the departure of the children of Israel was a work of God, in obedience to his express command, while yours from your Fatherland, was in many respects, I fear, a work of man, who deceived you with vain hopes of obtaining great things, extensive lands, rich property, etc. Some were indeed forced to emigrate, from their extreme necessities; but others, from needless, aye, I may say, sinful curiosity. As therefore, the beginning was mostly human, and in many instances sinful, so also the progress of events have shown that, for the most part, you have not reached the end you were seeking. Many are now contemplating a return to Germany, while to those who intend to go to the West Indies we wish only God's blessing.

"But there are more circumstances that enable me to speak of *The Similarity between your Journey and that of the Children of Israel in the Wilderness.* First, it was not without God's will, which often brings punishment and just judgment upon the world, that this has happened. Farther, beneath these chastisements, the goodness of God may be remarkably traced. You Palatines have many reasons for acknowledgment that God has wonderfully helped you thus far, and in a strange land has fed you with bread from Heaven, and refreshed you with water out of the rock, by opening the heart of our Most Gracious Queen, to bestow upon you such remarkable generosity, and awakening the sympathy and liberality of many of Her esteemed subjects. Nor should you forget that God did not leave you without pastors to care for your souls. A special Divine Providence has sustained you, like the children of Israel, so that in these extremely hard times, for many long months you have had all your wants supplied. Then, too, you are alike in the difficulty of the way, which you have experienced, and (God help you!) you must yet experience. Those who, like me, have looked after your interests, as both superintendents and servants, have had our sympathies and anxieties greatly exercised at the thought of the large number of people, for whom we had to care, with their many sicknesses and necessities, and miseries, from which many deaths, and other calamities have followed. Many alas! merited these punishments by their sins and vices. For your humiliation, I must say, that in nothing are you more like the children of Israel, than in your sins, your unbelief, your disobedience, your surroundings, your impatience, your discontent, your fleshy lusts, etc. No injustice would be done, if, like Moses, I were to call you an obstinate, and stiff-necked people, who walk after the thoughts of your hearts, and will not learn the ways of God, even when He has chastened you sore. For as you are like the children of Israel in your sins, so also are you in your punishments. This explains why it is that there are among you so many widows and widowers and orphans; although God has taken from you tender children, and provided for them far better than you ever attended.

"Now, why has God let all this come upon you? For this reason, says the text, 'to humble thee, and to prove thee, and to know what was in thy heart.' Many a one has thought that these intentions and purposes were the very best, who now sees, after God has thus proved him, that there was much that he lacked, that his former life was a failure, that he was seeking only earthly things, and was sinning grievously against God and his neighbor, and that he has been untrue even to himself. O that God would humble you, that you would fall at His feet, and heartily pray for forgiveness, and that He turn away the punishments you have heretofore experienced! * * * * *

"There is an anxiety that disturbs many with respect to their religion. They imagine that they cannot live in a land where they cannot attend public worship in their mother tongue. We would not depreciate the peculiar favor of God that preserves to one such a privilege. But where this is impossible, and one is well-grounded in his Christian faith, and in regard to all matters of faith there is freedom of conscience, no Christian should have any scruples of conscience about attending service in another language which he has learned, particularly if such service be held in Protestant and Evangelical churches. Such is the case with your friends in Ireland and elsewhere. A Christian proves all things, and holds fast to that which is good. We do not deny that in the so-called Christendom, the light of God's Word shines more brightly in one communion than another, and that we must not yield the least that concerns the pure and saving truth. But we oppose the fearful prejudices and false ideas of religion, that prevail to-day, and divide Christendom, and should not be judged otherwise than according to the meaning of Christ, 2 Cor. 4 : 20.

"Pray God, therefore, for grace and a true change of mind! Then will He regard your misery, and remove your want, and care for you both in body and in soul, and redeem you from all evil, and, after your pilgrimage has been finished in this sorrowful world He will at last grant to us all, who have placed our hopes upon Him, and have followed Him here, eternal peace, joy and salvation, through Jesus Christ, to Whom, with the Father and the Holy Ghost, be glory forever. *Amen*."

CHAPTER IV.—ON THE OCEAN.

HERE we may properly interrupt the narrative to consider some of the perils and hardships that were to be apprehended in the voyage. Many of them this company of emigrants were to suffer; but while they were spared from others, their countrymen who followed, the fathers of many of us, were not equally fortunate. Always uncertain was the length of the voyage. Pastor Kocherthal in his plea for Carolina, says that, when everything is favorable, the voyage from England thither could be made in six or five, and even, in exceptional cases, in four weeks; but that, under other circumstances, it might consume half a year. Before steam was used in navigation, the course might be interrupted by an indefinite calm. The imperfect knowl-

A "Compass rose," from an old chart.

edge of hydrography prevented them from taking advantage of well-defined ocean currents, and the lack of sufficient charts and light-houses rendered approach to the coast exceedingly difficult. The determination of the place of the ship, when compared with the results of the more exact methods of to-day, was scarcely more than guess-work. Men raised in our busy age would be worn out with the protracted delays of weeks and sometimes months, before the vessel in which they embarked, started, and would live over again the pains of Tantalus, while provoking calms kept the vessels from shore already seen, or contrary winds drove it far out to sea, after the goal of their long wandering had been almost attained.

The voyages of William Penn were made under the most favorable circumstances, and yet his first to America in 1682 consumed two months; his return in 1684, seven weeks; and his second trip to America in 1699, more than three months. Readers of Mr. Sachse's "History of the German Pietists," will recall the fact that the emigrants on the *Sarah Maria* were on board from February 13th to June 19th. More than a generation later, we find the Salzburgers making their way to the coast of Georgia, one transport leaving England at the very beginning of January, 1734, and reaching Charleston, March 18th (two months and a-half); and another leaving the coast of England, October 28, 1735, and reaching Charleston, February 15th, 1736 (three months and eighteen days). Henry Melchior Muhlenberg in 1742, left the coast of England, June 13th, and did not set foot upon solid land until September 23d, a voyage of three months and ten days. Pastor Handschuh, who arrived in 1748, went on board September 25, 1747, but because of an accident to the vessel, the final start was not taken until January 14th, and Philadelphia was not reached until April 5th, six months and ten days from the time of embarkation.

With half the shipping engaged in illegitimate business, as smuggling, privateering and piracy, the risk of sailing without a convoy of men-of-war was great, while the difficulty of securing them was another source of vexatious delays. Cases of piracy and mutiny are frequent subjects of consideration in the Minutes of the Provincial Council of Pennsylvania. The coasts of the Carolinas and Georgia were favorite lurking places for pirates.

Their exploits have been recounted in a monograph published a few years ago under the authority of Johns Hopkins' University: "*The Carolina Pirates* and *Colonial Commerce*, 1670–1740," 1894. Beginning as privateers against the Spanish dominions in America, not only with the authority, but the very decided encouragement of King Charles II., the trade was so well learned by a host of adventurers, that when peace between the two countries came, their efforts were directed towards an illegitimate continuance of the same work. The doubtful compliment of Scaliger shows the extent of this crime in the English colonies: "*Nulli melius piraticam exercent quam Angli.*" It is alleged that for years their chief victims were still Spanish, and that, in this course, they were not without

Blackbeard the Pirate.
(From a contemporary print.)

much sympathy from the inhabitants of the Southern colonies, as they looked upon them as some protection against the dread of a violation of treaty rights by the Spanish. However this may be, the pirates did not scruple long about preying upon whatever commerce was within reach, without regard to the flag under which it floated. During the administration of Governor Craven, 1711–13, it was estimated that no less than 1,500 men engaged in this business, infested the coast. Of these 800 had their headquarters on the island of Providence, while the mouth of the Cape Fear River was the next chief place of resort. " They swept the coast from Newfoundland to South America, plundering their prizes at sea, or carrying them into Cape Fear or Providence as best suited their convenience."[1] In June, 1718, Edward Thatch (Teach) known as "Blackbeard," appeared off Charleston, with four vessels, the largest of forty guns, and with four hundred men in his fleet, and remaining there for days, captured all the vessels entering or going from the harbor. Sending a boat to Charleston, he forced the Governor of South Carolina, to furnish him with necessary medical supplies, under the menace of the execution of certain prominent citizens whom he had captured. Thatch, whose depredations extended to the approaches to Philadelphia, was captured shortly after this bold move by an expedition sent against him by Governor Spottswood, of Virginia.

---

[1] Interesting details in " *The History of South Carolina under the Proprietory Government,*" by Edward MacCrady, New York, 1897, especially Chapters XXVI. and XXVII.

"Hardly a ship goes to sea," writes the Governor of South Carolina, " but falls into the hands of pirates."

Major Stede Bonnet, a man of liberal education, good family and wealth with a creditable military record, was led, by some strange infatuation, after he had passed the prime of life, to embark in this same career of crime, and to rival Thatch in the terror he struck along the entire Atlantic coast. In the summer of 1718, he took thirty-eight vessels, among them several in the Delaware Bay. On September 27, 1718, a desperate naval battle was fought at Cape Fear by two vessels despatched thither, under Col. William Rhett, by the Governor of South Carolina, and the ship of Bonnet. He and his men were captured, but not until after five hours hard fighting, and the loss by the Carolinians of twelve killed and twenty-eight wounded. Their trial had scarcely begun before the alarm was sounded that another body of pirates was at the entrance of Charleston Harbor. Hastily fitting up another expedition, in which the vessel captured from Bonnet was utilized, the Governor undertook the command in person, and went forth with four vessels and twenty-eight guns. The pirates were surprised, and captured, but only after a battle almost equally severe to that at Cape Fear. In one of their two ships, were found 106 convicts and " covenant servants," en route to Maryland and Virginia, whom the pirates were holding as prisoners. Worley the piratical chief killed in this engagement, is said to have terrorized the coasts in the vicinity of New York and Philadelphia. In November,

86 *The Pennsylvania-German Society.*

1718, there were in Charleston no less than forty-five pirates executed.

In the first volume of " *The American Weekly Mercury*," the first paper published in the City of Philadelphia, and which is being rendered accessible by the photographic reproduction of our skillful fellow-member, Julius F.

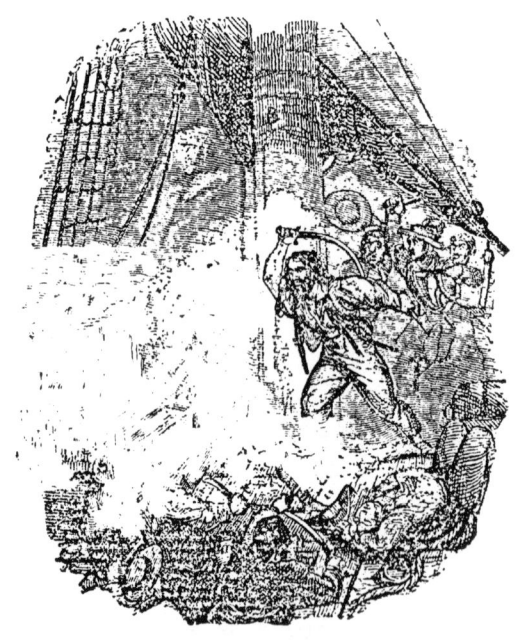

A Battle with Pirates.

Sachse, the accounts of the depredations of pirates, from Newfoundland to Brazil, are prominent items of news. May 17, 1720, tells of the capture of a certain Capt. Knot, with his vessel by 148 pirates, who was released, but compelled to take on board as passengers eight men, who conveyed in this way their treasure of 1,500 pounds sterling to Virginia, but were there arrested and hung. April 7th, a ship has just arrived in New York, that had been robbed by pirates in the Barbadoes. April 14th, a Philadelphia vessel has been robbed on her way to the Barbadoes. May 5th, an engagement with pirates off the Barbadoes, in which they escape. Rescue of a vessel from pirates, near Boston. May 19th, Capt. Thorpe of Philadelphia, captured by Spanish privateers, off the capes of Virginia. June 30th, account of depredations on the coasts of Guinea. July 14th, Spanish privateers and pirates on the Virginia capes. Release of 70 prisoners taken by them. Corpses of those they had killed discovered. September 1st, capture of a ship by a pirate off the banks of Newfoundland. Ten thousand pounds sterling thrown overboard. Rumor that the Fort of St. John has been taken by pirates, and all the fishing vessels there destroyed. September 8th, the brigantine "Essex" reaches Salem, after being captured by pirates, sixty leagues east of the banks of Newfoundland by two vessels, one of 25 guns and 100 men, and the other of 10 guns. Just before this capture another vessel had fallen into their hands. September 22d relates a feat of remarkable audacity. Pirates in a small sloop of 12 guns, and with 160 men had entered Trespassy, and taken possession of the harbor with all the vessels there, including 22 sail. The ship carpenters were pressed into the work of making such repairs as the pirates desired. Thirty French and English ships had been destroyed on the banks. The week before, they had been at Ferryland, where two

ARTICLES of Agreement, made this 10th day of October in the Year of our Lord 1695. between the Right Honourable Richard Earl of Bellomont of the one part, and Robert Levingston Esq; and Capt. William Kid of the other part.

WHEREAS the said Capt. *William Kid* is desirous of obtaining a Commission as Captain of a Private Man of War in order to take Prizes from the King's Enemies, and otherways to annoy them; and whereas certain Persons did some time since depart from *New-England, Rode-Island, New-York*, and other parts in *America* and elsewhere, with an intention to become Pirates, and to commit Spoils and Depredations, against the Laws of Nations, in the *Red-Sea* or elsewhere, and to return with such Goods and Riches as they should get, to certain places by them agreed upon; of which said Persons and Places the said Capt. *Kid* hath notice, and is desirous to fight with and subdue the said Pirates, as also all other Pirates with whom

---

Facsimile of heading of the original Broadside, now in collection of the Historical Society of Pennsylvania

vessels were burnt. Although they had had two days' notice of their approach, and there were in the harbor 1,200 men, with 40 guns, all were paralyzed with fear, and unable to make a resistance. Other notices of depredations are recorded on October 27th, November 10th, November 24th, and December 8th.

The evil must have been indeed extreme, when in 1697, Penn wrote to Deputy Governor Markham of Pennsylvania charging the Provincial Council with having "not only countenanced, but actually encouraged piracy." The Council indignantly protested that no piratical vessels had ever been harbored, much less encouraged in Pennsylvania, and make a public proclamation announcing the charge, and urging all magistrates to prove its incorrectness by a rigid enforcement of the laws guarding against such offence. On Penn's return, we are told that his first act on reassuming control of the government, was to reconvene the Assembly "for the express and only purpose of reënacting two measures, which in his opinion, the existing state of affairs rendered imperative." The first of these was "An Act against Pirates and Privateers."[1]

The notorious depredations of Capt. Kidd extended into the Delaware Bay. Penn's charge against the Provincial Council must be read in the light of the fact that Kidd had embarked upon his career as a privateersman with a commission from the Governor of New York, the Earl of Bella-

---

[1] *Duke of York's Laws*, etc. Harrisburg, 1879. Historical Notes on Early Government and Legislative Councils by Benjamin W. Nead, pp. 573 sqq.

Page from Muhlenberg's Diary of Voyage in 1742. (In Archives of Theological Seminary, Mt. Airy, Philadelphia.)

THE PENNSYLVANIA-GERMAN SOCIETY.

Henry Melchior Muhlenberg

mont, who had to meet the charge that his appointment as Governor was determined by his purpose to encourage piracy. It was the irony of fate that Kidd was to be condemned and executed in 1700[1] under Bellamy himself. Indignant as were his protests that he was guiltless of encouraging piracy, the commission of 1697 tells its own tale.

While on his way to England in 1718, to present the grievances of the Palatines, John Conrad Weiser, Sr., was captured shortly after leaving Philadelphia, and most cruelly handled. The same year King George I. made a proclamation, offering an amnesty to all pirates abandoning their trade. One of the most interesting incidents in Mr. Sachse's book is the description by Daniel Falkner[2] of the sea fight with the three French vessels during the voyage hither of German pietists in 1694. Mr. Brickenstein, in his account of the First Sea Congregation of the Moravians, has given a graphic description of the manner in which an attack of a privateer was repulsed by the forty-nine hats of peaceful and unarmed brethren seen upon the deck. A similar ruse was attempted by the vessel that brought Muhlenberg to this country in 1742, when cannon were loaded and the drummers beat their drums. We present a facsimile of a page of his diary where he refers to this incident:

---

[1] See *Commission;* also *Full Account of Proceedings against Capt. Cook,* London, 170.

[2] The finding of the original manuscript in the archives at Halle, shows that this report was written by Johann Gottfried Seelig, a former Secretary to Rev. Philip Jacob Spener, who came over with the Kelpins community, and not by Falkner, as has been heretofore assumed.—J. F SACHSE.

"It was a Spaniard. But we heard nothing more. The merchant's vessel beat off from us, and so far outran us, that by evening we no longer saw anything of it, and were alone. In the afternoon we had fine weather and little wind. Towards evening, the captain ordered that every male person in the vessel should come on the quarter deck and drill. Nothing was said to me. About five o'clock they all came together, received their sabres, pistols, muskets, guns and powder. A tailor, one of the passengers, had, out of fear, concealed himself in the hold. Him they drew out with a rope. Thereupon the captain showed each one the place where he should stand, in case a hostile attack should be made. They drilled for several hours and fired. The smell of powder freshened me up a little, so that in the evening I could, for the first time in the week, eat a bit with an appetite. On July 11th, it being the fourth Sunday after Trinity, I held divine service with the Salzburgers, and we greatly refreshed ourselves from the Gospel of Luke 6, so that we were able to rejoice in our Saviour. The captain and several Englishmen. [1]

The imminence of this danger to the Palatines, in this and subsequent voyages, may be inferred from the scheme that may still be read, prepared in 1711 for Gov. Hunter for guarding the coasts "against the insults of French privateers," in which they are designated as "swarms which every summer infest our coasts, where they not only take vast numbers of our vessels, but have plundered several small towns and villages."

---

[1] From the diary of Muhlenberg, while on his voyage to America, 1742.

The long voyages rendered it difficult to carry sufficient provisions and to keep them in good condition. Contractors were no less dishonest in those days than in our own, and where the emigrants were carried at the lowest figures every effort was made to economize in the quality and quantity of the food. Extraordinary delays meant hunger, if not starvation. The bill of fare, with meat four times, and fish three times a week, recorded by Pastorius, as that of the vessel in which he sailed, bears a wonderful contrast with that of a Cunarder or North German Lloyd of to-day; but when his passage was only six pounds sterling for himself, and twenty-two rix-dollars for each domestic, he received an equivalent for what he paid.[1] Often the drinking water failed. Muhlenberg's description of the eagerness of the passengers on his vessel to catch a few drops of rain from passing showers; of the rush of the children to collect the water escaping from the joints of the casks just received from a passing ship, and the desperate ingenuity of the rats when they emptied the vinegar bottles by drawing the corks and using their tails as absorbents of the precious fluid, give some impression of the extremity to which emigrants were sometimes put.[2]

Often the captains and sailors were rough, domineering, cruel, and emigrants were crowded in with vermin-covered and profane fellow-passengers. Pastor Handschuh speaks of those with whom he sailed being packed together like herring. "Like herring," also Muhlenberg says, the

[1] Pastorius, *Beschreibung von Pennsyl.*, Crefeld, 1884. (Reprint.)
[2] Mann's *Life of H. M. Mühlenberg*, Philadelphia, 1887, pp. 48 sqq.

people slept in the cabin of the packet that carried him from Savannah to Philadelphia. Casper Wistar writes in 1732 of a ship that had been twenty-four weeks at sea, that had lost one hundred of its one hundred and fifty passengers by starvation, the rats and mice having been caught to satisfy the hunger, and the price of a mouse fixed at half a gulden, and whose survivors were all thrown into prison for the debts of the living and the dead.[1] Another vessel, seventeen weeks on the way, lost sixty of its passengers, and brought the rest to land in a condition of extreme enfeeblement. The experience of the Palatines, wrecked on the coast of Virginia in 1717, has been already related. In December, 1738, a ship was wrecked at Block Island, that had sailed with four hundred Palatines, all of whom save one hundred and five had died of fever, while fifteen more died shortly after landing, the entire loss being over seventy-seven per cent., and the bad condition of the water taken in at Rotterdam being assigned as the cause of the mortality. Fifty survivors out of four hundred, the most of the deaths having been from starvation, was the record of a vessel that arrived at Philadelphia in 1745. Bread had been distributed every two weeks in such scant amounts that many consumed it in less than half the time it was intended to last, when, if they had money, they bought meal and wine at exorbitant rates, but, otherwise, were left to their fate. The deaths in fifteen vessels in 1738, are estimated by one writer as sixteen hundred, while

---

[1] Letter in *Sammlung Ausserlessener Materiel zum Bau des Reichs Gottes*, Leipzig, 1733, Vol. IX. p. 512.

Christopher Saur regards two thousand no exaggeration. On the ship that carried Henry Keppele that year two hundred and fifty died, exclusive of the victims of the voyage after landing.

With no attention paid to the sanitation of ships, ship fever was no unusual scourge. A medical commission appointed by the Provincial Council of Pennsylvania in 1754, made a full report concerning the diseases produced and propagated from the overcrowded vessels of Palatines, as follows:

> "The diseases to which all places are liable from foreigners brought among them in crowded vessels are: first, fevers from a foul air, which is common to these ships; secondly, these fevers aggravated by other causes on board the ships or in houses where too many of the sick have been kept together in small and close rooms; thirdly, fevers from infectious matter brought on board the ships from other places. That you may be the better able to judge of the means necessary for preventing these diseases, we think it will not be improper first to say something of their causes, and then to show by facts where the danger of infection from them lies.
>
> "The steam of bilge water and the breath of great numbers of people betwixt the decks of a ship make the air moist and in some degree putrid, and, like that of moist and boggy places, will produce fevers on persons that are a long time in them, but these fevers are not contagious and require no other precaution, but separating the sick and keeping them in places well aired and cleaned.

"But when to this state of the air, any considerable degree of animal putrefaction is added, either from uncleanness, flukes, etc., or too great a confinement of the air itself, it then produces a fever different in its symptoms from the former, malignant in its nature and contagious. Military hospitals afford us daily instances of the mildest fevers being by these causes changed into malignant and contagious ones, and prove how dangerous it is for many sick persons to be kept together in the manner we found the Palatines in the two houses mentioned to you in our last report. But the most fatal circumstances attending contagious fevers are when persons infected by them in jails and other places (where the cause has been long gaining force) communicate them to the passengers of a crowded ship in the beginning of a summer voyage, where, from the number of the sick, heat of the weather and frequent calms, they rage with such violence and continue so long that every part of the ship imbibes the poison, and will retain it for a considerable time, after both goods and people have been taken out of her. The vessels of this port that bring people from these places usually land them in a neighboring government and have not been sufficiently suspected of danger as we are persuaded the following facts will convince you:

"Captain Arthur, who was then a mate of Captain Davis, told us that in the year 1741 they took in a parcel of convicts from the Dublin Gaol and other servants from the city. Soon after the people on board were seized with fevers, which few escaped, so that they were in great distress from the number of the sick during the whole voyage. Where the people were landed we did not inquire; but this ship, after they were out, was brought to Hamilton's wharf, and from thence carried to Thomas Penrose's to be repaired. Soon after her coming to the wharf seven persons in the family of Anthony Morris, the elder, and several in the house of Anthony Morris, the younger, were seized with putrid bilious fever, and seventeen of Mr. Penrose's family who had been on board the ship, were likewise affected with the same fever, and also sundry persons in every part of that neighborhood where the ballast of the ship was thrown. This fever afterwards raged through the city to the loss of many of its valuable inhabitants.

* * * * * * * * *

"Ever since the middle of September there have been a few putrid fevers in this city, which we believe were not owing to the climate but to an infection either brought or generated among us by foreigners. The first of these certainly did not come from the Palatines, but whether they have added fresh fuel and continued them, we cannot determine: however this, we are convinced of (and which we have never till lately suspected) that the true state of the Palatine ships is too often concealed from the physicians who visit them, in such a manner that it is impossible to discover it from anything they can see on board.

"There have been diseases of the same nature with these mentioned at other times in the city, but we did not know anything relating to them that would make their enumeration necessary; therefore, shall conclude with only taking the liberty to assure you we are,

"Sir, Your most obedient humble servants,

"THOMAS GREEME,
"THOMAS BOND.

"December 2, 1754."

To this is added the melancholy postscript:

"The Council, for their further information, sent for Jacob Shoemaker, the man who has the care of the Strangers' Burying Ground, and ordered him to deliver in upon oath the number of Palatines buried there, which he did as follows:

"An account of the Palatines buried this year:

"For Alexander Stedman........ 62
"For Henry Keppelly........... 39
"For Benjamin Shoemaker...... 57
"For Daniel Benezet........... 87
"For Michael Hillegass......... 8
"Total.................... ...253

"Jacob Shoemaker upon his affirmation saith the above account of burials since the 14th of September last is exact and true from his book and the account of coffins, except those from Michael Hillegass, which he thinks may be six or eight more, and some to be buried this day, November 14, 1754."[1]

This indicates that the average mortality of Palatines just arrived, at the port of Philadelphia, continued throughout an entire summer to be from eight to nine per day.

Nevertheless, it must not be inferred that such was the universal experience of the emigrant vessels. Instances are on record where vessels filled with German emigrants brought every passenger to land; but the mortality from small-pox on the ship in which William Penn came hither in 1682, shows that the utmost precautions could not entirely exclude such perils. Well has the late Dr. Mann,

---
[1] *Pennsylvania Colonial Records*, VI., 173 sqq.

Henry Keppele

in his "Life of Muhlenberg," designated the vessels of those days, as instead of the floating palaces of to-day, being "combinations of floating fortresses, floating prisons and floating hospitals."

Such trustworthy witnesses as John Wesley, Baron von Reck, Pastor Boltzius of the Salzburgers and Henry Melchior Muhlenburg have given graphic descriptions of the numerous, fierce and protracted storms they encountered, and the varied conduct of the passengers in the presence of danger, as the prospect of immediate death, while sails were tearing and masts breaking and the vessel giving every indication that all was lost, unmanned the bravest and called forth shrieks of horror from some, but still others, elsewhere most timid, met the crisis with an indescribable composure, arising from their conviction that their Father in Heaven held the waves of the sea in the hollow of His hands. It was such heaven-born peace, displayed by his German fellow-passengers, that astonished Wesley, and, according to his own confession, led him to an entirely new conception of the Christian life.

Rev. John Wesley's Journal.[1]

"*Saturday, January 17, 1736.*—Many people were very impatient at the contrary wind. At seven in the evening they were quieted by a storm. It rose higher and higher till nine. About nine the sea broke over us from stem to stern; burst through the windows of the state cabin, where three or four of us

---

[1] The works of Rev. John Wesley, M.A., London, 1829, I., 20–23.

were, and covered us all over, though a bureau sheltered me from the main shock. About eleven I lay down in the great cabin, and in a short time fell asleep, though very uncertain whether I should wake alive, and much ashamed of my unwillingness to die. O how pure in heart must he be, who would rejoice to appear before God at a moment's warning! Toward morning, ' He rebuked the winds and the sea, and there was a great calm.'

" *Sunday 18.*—We returned God thanks for our deliverance, of which a few seemed duly sensible. But the rest (among whom were most of the sailors) denied we had been in any danger. I could not have believed that so little good would have been done by the terror they were in before. But it cannot be that they should long obey God from fear, who are deaf to the motives of love.

" *Friday 23.*—In the evening another storm began, in the morning it increased, so that they were forced to let the ship drive. I could not but say to myself, ' How is it that thou hast no faith?' being still unwilling to die. About one in the afternoon, almost as soon as I had stepped out of the great cabin door, the sea did not break as usual, but came with a full, smooth tide over the side of the ship. I was vaulted over with water in a moment, and so stunned, that I scarce expected to lift up my head again, till the sea should give up her dead. But thanks be to God, I received no hurt at all. About midnight the storm ceased.

" *Sunday 25.*—At noon our third storm began. At four it was more violent than before. Now, indeed, we could say, ' The waves of the sea were mighty, and raged horribly. They rose up to the heavens above,' and clave 'down to hell beneath.' The winds roared round about us, and (what I never heard before) whistled as distinctly as if it had been a human voice. The ship not only rocked to and fro with the utmost violence, but shook and jarred with so unequal, grating a motion, that one could not but with great difficulty keep one's hold of anything, nor stand a moment without it. Every ten minutes came a shock against the stern or side of the ship, which one would think should dash the planks in pieces. At this time a child, privately baptized before, was brought to be received into the church. It put me in mind of Jeremiah's buying the field when the Chaldeans were on the point of destroying Jerusalem, and seemed a pledge of the mercy God designed to show us, even in the land of the living.

"We spent two or three hours after prayers in conversing suitably to the occasion, confirming one another in a calm submission to the wise, holy, gracious will of God. And now a storm did not seem so terrible as before. Blessed be the God of all consolation!

"At seven I went to the Germans. I had long before observed the great seriousness of their behaviour. Of their humility they had given a continual proof, by performing those servile offices for the other passengers, which none of the English would undertake; for which they desired, and would receive no pay, saying, "it was good for their proud hearts," and "their loving Saviour had done more for them." And every day had given them occasion of showing a meekness, which no injury could move. If they were pushed, struck, or thrown down, they rose again and went away; but no complaint was found in their mouth. There was now an opportunity of trying whether they were delivered from the spirit of fear, as well as from that of pride, anger, and revenge. In the midst of the psalm wherewith their service began, the sea broke over, split the main-sail in pieces, covered the ship, and poured in between the decks as if the great deep had already swallowed us up. A terrible screaming began among the English. The Germans calmly sung on. I asked one of them afterwards, 'Were you not afraid?' He answered, 'I thank my God, no.' I asked, 'But were not your women and children afraid?' He replied, mildly, 'No, our women and children are not afraid to die.'

"From them I went to their crying, trembling neighbors and pointed out to them the difference in the hour of trial, between him that feareth God, and him that feareth him not. At twelve the wind fell. This was the most glorious day which I have hitherto seen.

"*Monday 26.*—We enjoyed the calm. I can conceive no difference, comparable to that between a smooth and a rough sea, except that which is between a mind calmed by the love of God, and one torn up by the storms of earthly passions.

"*Thursday 29.*—About seven in the evening, we fell in with the skirts of a hurricane. The rain as well as the wind was extremely violent. The sky was so dark in a moment that the sailors could not so much as see the ropes, or set about furling the sails. The ship must, in all probability, have overset, had not the wind fell as suddenly as it rose. Toward the end of it, we had that appearance on each of the masts, which (it is thought) the ancients called Castor and Pollux.

A Religious Leader. 103

Schaitberger, the religious leader of the Salzburgers.

It was a small ball of white fire like a star. The mariners say it appears either in a storm (and then commonly upon the deck), or just at the end of it, and then it is usually on the masts or sails.

"*Friday 30.*—We had another storm, which did us no other harm than splitting the foresail. Our bed being wet, I laid me down on the floor, and slept sound till morning. And I believe I shall not find it needful to go to bed (as it is called) any more.

"*Sunday, February 1.*—We spoke with a ship of Carolina; and Wednesday 4, came within sounding. About noon, the trees were visible from the masts, and in the afternoon from the main deck. In the evening lesson were these words; "A great door, and effectual, is opened." O let no one shut it!

"*Thursday 5.*—Between two and three in the afternoon God brought us all safe into the Savannah river."

"VON RECK'S JOURNAL.[1]
1736.

"*January 31.*—A great Shower of Rain fell and the Wind changed to WEST. Thus God confounds the Opinions of Men, and convinces them that He is Almighty and Master of the Winds; for the Sailors, who had persuaded us that the Trade-Wind blew constantly from the same Quarter, found now the contrary.

"*February 6.*—At Night a tempestuous Wind arose, but God in his Goodness held his Almighty hand over

---

[1] *An Extract of the Journal of Mr. Commissary Von Reck.* Published by direction of the Society for Promoting Christian Knowledge, London, 1734. Reprinted in Force's *Historical Tracts*, Washington, 1846. Vol. IV., Nos. 5, 6, 7.

us, and was pleased the next Day to give us a good Wind, which advanced us five or six Miles an Hour.

"*February 16.*—At Two in the Afternoon the Wind turned contrary N. by W., but being very gentle, the Sea was calm all that Night. It is remarkable that hitherto the contrary Winds have always been gentle, and immediately followed by a calm, so that we never went back.

"*February 17.*—We had this Evening at Prayers PSALM I, 14. OFFER UNTO GOD THANKSGIVING AND PAY THY VOWS UNTO THE MOST HIGHEST; Which we heartily did, for all his loving Mercies vouchsafed unto us; and at the same time, we Vowed a Vow, as JACOB did in GEN. 28 and the 20th Verse.

"*February 18.*—At two in the afternoon the Wind was strong at S., and soon after it proved contrary, and extremely violent. I was very much surprised to see the Sea rise so high; a Tempest darkened the Sky; the Waves swelled and foamed; and everything threatened to overwhelm us in the Deep. All the Sails were furled; the violence of the wind was so great that it tore the Main Sail in pieces. Besides which, the Mate cried out that the Water rose fast in the Hold; but though he spoke Truth, the Ship received no damage. We sighed, we cried unto God, and prayed him to help us. He heard and comforted us by some Passages of the Holy Scripture, as ISA. 51, 15, PSAL. 39, 7, 8, JOB chap. 14 and 17.

"*February 20.*—We saw a Scotch Ship, bound for Charles-town, and soon lost sight of her again.

"*February 27.*—Last night we had the Wind contrary W.S.W., but God Granted us a sweet Repose and renewed our Strength, the better to undergo a

Tempest, which a wind at W. by S. brought upon us by Break of Day. This storm was more dreadful than the other. One sees always death present in a Storm, and is more sensibly convinced of this Truth, that there may be but a moment between Life and Death. Wherefore those who are not thoroughly converted to God, and assured of the happiness of the Life to come, are the most miserable at Sea, for if they chance to perish, they perish in their sins. We made the Holy Scriptures our Refuge, some Passages whereof did mightily comfort us, as ISA. 54, 7, 8, and the following Verses, LUK. 18, 7, 8, HEB. v. 7, MIC. 7, v. 18. Divine Mercy preserved us through our Saviour, and at night the Wind abated."

The Palatine emigration of 1710 did not escape all these perils. The younger Weiser estimates the mortality on the voyage and immediately after as seventeen hundred, and his father and Scheff, in their petitions to the Board of Trade, August 2, 1720, give the same figure as that of those who "died on board, or at their landing by unavoidable sickness." But as they fix the number of emigrants as four thousand, the discrepancy in the records of the mortality is based upon the discrepancy in the record of the entire company. Governor Hunter reported immediately after his arrival: "The poor people have been mighty sickly, but recover apace. We have lost about four hundred and seventy of our number." One vessel was yet to be heard from. Two hundred and fifty are reported as having died of ship fever shortly after landing. The official report made by Mr. Du Pre to the Board of

THE PENNSYLVANIA-GERMAN SOCIETY.

*Your Affectionate Servant
John Wesley*

Trade, January 6, 1711, gives the number of survivors, when he left New York, probably in October, as 2,227. As Boehme's figures of 3,086, as the number of those who embarked, seem to be accurate, the entire loss was 859, of whom 609, or twenty per cent. of the company died on the voyage. In his petition in 1720, Scheff declares that the Palatines "lost most of their young children at their going from home to America." Boehme states that those packed in the lowest parts of the vessels were without fresh air and sunlight, and, under these circumstances, the small and tender children among them generally died. "Of some families, neither parents nor children survive." In one ship eighty died, and one hundred more were lying sick at one time. The causes assigned are two: first, the crowded condition of the vessels, and, secondly, the merciless treatment of the captains, who did not provide good and wholesome food. They landed a crushed, sick and dispirited band of exiles, after a voyage of about six months, as the vessels came in irregularly and differed in the exact time of the passage. One of them, *The Herbert*, was grounded on the coast of Long Island, July 7th, twenty-one days after the first came to shore. "The men are safe," writes Hunter, "but the goods are much damaged." The tenth vessel, *The Berkley Castle*, on July 24, was six weeks overdue; although its later start from Plymouth must be taken into account. The grounding of *The Herbert* has been made the basis for a romantic story and a beautiful poem by Whittier. Local tradition had told of a vessel called *The Palatine*, that was lured by false lights upon the rocks and then robbed and its passengers murdered. Certain graves, said to be those of Palatines, traceable in the vicinity, are referred to as evidences of the truth of the story. Governor Hunter's statement that the men were safe is interpreted as referring only to the English on board. But, as *The Herbert* according to Hunter carried all the arms and tents of the expedition, and the goods on board were reported only as much damaged, any attack upon them or any acts of piracy would have been related. Nor would he have been so indifferent to the murder of some of the Palatines, when in his despatch he speaks sympathizingly of their sickness at sea, and his mind was so intent upon plans in which he hoped to derive great gain from the industry of every colonist. They may have been wrecked by false lights; but if so the hopes of the wreckers were blasted by the force that they found that they would encounter. The poet, however, has pictured the details of the plot to its consummation:

> " Old wives spinning their webs of tow,
> Or rocking weirdly to and fro
> In and out of the peat's dull glow,

> " And old men mending their nets of twine,
> Talk together of dream and sign,
> Talk of the lost ship *Palatine*;

> " The ship that a hundred years before,
> Freighted deep with its goodly store,
> In the gales of the equinox went ashore.

> " The eager islanders one by one,
> Counted the shots of her signal gun,
> And heard the crash when she drove right on!

"Into the teeth of death she sped:
(May God forgive the hands that fed
The false lights over the rocky Head).

"O men and brothers! what sights were there!
White upturned faces, hands stretched out in prayer!
Where waves had pity, could ye not spare?

"Down swooped the wreckers, like birds of prey
Tearing the heart of the ship away,
And the dead had never a word to say.

"And then with ghastly shimmer and shine
Over the rocks and the seething brine,
They burned the wreck of the *Palatine*."

The foundation of truth in the tradition may have been the wreck of a Palatine vessel at some later time, that in some way was diverted from its course to Pennsylvania. The prayers of the band whose history we have been recounting for protection from such perils were heard. They had trials enough before as well as behind them to be spared such a calamity.

CHAPTER V.—IN NEW YORK.

ON landing at New York, they were sent to Nuttal's, now Governor's Island, then the quarantine station, to be nursed and recruited for still further trials. To lessen the burden of providing for them, the children fit for service were bound out, an expedient, which, however, justifiable, separated families in a time of distress, as the hand of death had already fallen heavily upon them, and practically enslaved some who in Germany had been reared in homes that had never known want.

Meanwhile Hunter proceeded to the execution of his visionary schemes that he had projected in England. His plans for accumulating extensive revenues through the services of the Palatines were as unpractical as Brad-

Seal of Province of New York.

A STREET SCENE IN NEW YORK, 1709.
FROM AN OLD SKETCH.

dock's subsequent military campaigns against the Indians. The responsibility for the care of the immigrants lay upon him. When the appropriations, made upon his estimate of necessities, were exhausted, he did not hesitate to devote his private resources to the support of the people, and soon found them insufficient. The Palatines, on the other hand, finding the promises made them unfulfilled, and understanding, for the first time, the full meaning of the pledge they had made in England, regarded him as their enemy and defrauder. To add to these perplexities, the Provincial Council of New York disputed the right of the Crown to pay Hunter's salary from the income of the Province. Some sympathy must be felt for a man thus in the center of a triangular fire, especially in the extremity in which he wrote, four years later, to the Lord High Treasurer of England, that he must continue to throw himself at His Lordship's feet, until he kicked him away, and must beg for but one-fourth of the Palatines' debts to stop the mouths of clamorous creditors.

In one year, according to Hunter's reckoning, the Palatines should have been able to subsist themselves, and, after that, a prompt return was to be made for the amount that the Government had expended for their transportation and maintenance. In the autumn of 1710, some 1,500 were, therefore, taken up the Hudson to the lands of Robert Livingstone, from whom 6,000 acres were at once purchased for 266 English pounds sterling, while 800 additional acres were purchased the following spring, and 6,333 acres, on the other side of the Hudson, were also utilized. On the eastern side, three towns were laid out, the entire district being known as East Camp; while the two towns on the west side constituted West Camp. Each family was provided with a lot forty feet front and fifty feet deep. An additional village soon sprang up on each side. Large pine forests were in the immediate vicinity.

The Founding of a Home in the New World.

When all were quartered, the Lords of the Treasury received rose-colored reports from Hunter. "The great project," he wrote, "could not fail of success. 15,000 pounds a year for the next two years, would do the work effectually. Her Majesty might depend upon tar enough for her navy from her colonies forever; for there was

An Early Church.

The Old Quassaick Church. Built during the ministration of Rev. Michael Christian Knoll.

pitch pine enough, if the number of hands was employed, to serve all Europe."

But the Board of Trade was not satisfied. Mr. Du Pre, the Commissary, was summoned before them and examined, as to why the Governor wanted subsistence for the Palatines for more than one year, as at first proposed. Then came out the stern facts "that the first year may be looked upon as lost, because of the usual hard weather prevailing there in the winter; and that, in the second year, the time would be insufficient to clear the ground and to raise enough grain for their subsistence, and in the third year, a great portion of their labor would be devoted to preparing the trees for the manufacture of tar."

The prospect became still darker when more was learned of the process of manufacture. For two years, the trees had to be treated before being available for the purpose. Finland tar, the best in the market, it was discovered, was selling for four shillings a barrel, one-half of the price upon which Governor Hunter had calculated, when estimating the money productivity of the Palatines.

But Hunter hoped against hope. He would not admit his mistake. Even in 1712, he writes most encouragingly of the progress made, and that 100,000 trees were ready to be cut for tar. His one difficulty, he complains, is that of bearing alone the heavy pecuniary responsibility imposed upon him. He had gone on, he says, laying out all the money he and his friends were masters of, for subsisting and employing that people, but had not heard that any of his bills were paid. He had reaped nothing but fatigue, torture and trouble, and the pleasure of having surmounted opposition and difficulties next to insurmountable. There was no revenue to support his government, the frontiers were exposed, and "the Indians, though but a handful, were saucy, while the officers of the Government were all a starving."

R. Livingston

The man who profited by the transaction seems to have been Livingstone. The Earl of Clarendon describes him as "a very ill man," who had practiced extensive frauds on the Government, and laments that Hunter has fallen into his hands. Reference to the commission of Capt. Kidd printed on a preceding page (see above p. 88) shows that the partner with Lord Bellamont in sending Kidd out as privateer was "Robert Livingston, Esq."

The Palatines were indignant that, without consulting them, Hunter should make with Livingstone terms, according to which they were ultimately to pay the latter. The great mistake of the English Government throughout, had been, that it dealt with these people *en masse*, or as a community, and not as individuals; and, that in its measures for their relief, instead of treating them as impoverished freemen, it virtually enslaved them. An assertion of their rights was inevitable. Not unwilling to work, and ready, upon equitable terms, to repay all that had been expended for them, they asked only that each individual should receive the rewards of his own toil. Having taken the oath of allegiance, they endeavored to conduct themselves as loyal, law-abiding citizens, as their cheerful participation in the expedition against Montreal in 1711 under General Nicholson, and their subsequent response to the appeal for the defence of Albany, when it was threatened by the French and Indians, testify. In the Canadian campaign, John Conrad Weiser, Hartman Weinbecker and John Peter Kneskern were the captains. On each of these occasions, the Palatines furnished three hundred soldiers. As six hundred was the quota of the Province of New York for this expedition, although it was somewhat enlarged, the Palatine contingent distributed in the regiments of Colonels Schuyler and Ingoldsbey formed a very large proportion of the army. If Hunter's statement of the resolution of the Assembly of New York be correct, the Palatines were not treated with proper respect in the action, by which the Province proposed at first to raise as its quota "three hundred and fifty Christians, one hundred and fifty Long Island Indians, and one hundred Palatines!" While the statement of the number furnished as three hundred is official and is mentioned by the authorities several times, the rosters that have been preserved are incomplete. But the names of the men, who, notwithstanding the injustice under which they were suffering and protesting, were ready, one year after their arrival, to respond to the call to defend their adopted country, are worthy of preservation. Among them are the ancestors of many Pennsylvania Germans.

"*From Queensberry:* John Conrad Weiser, Captain; Christian Haber, Andreas Bergman, Johannis Feeg, Mattheus Kuntz, Mattheus Reinbolt, Joh. Peter Dopff, John Jacob Reisch, Carl Nehr, Henrich Jung, Hen. Hoffman, Werner Deichert, George Mueller, Fred. Bellenger, Hen. Widerwachs, Geo. Mathias, Christo. Hagedorn, Frantz Finck, Andreas Schurtz, Peter Hagedorn, Niclaus Weber, Wm. George, Lieut., Fred. Schaffer, Anth. Ichard, John Peter Sein, John Jacob Munsinger, Johan Leyer, Jacob Kuhn, Hen. Mathous, Nicklaus Eckard, Martin Dilleback, Niclaus Feller, Jacob Schnell, Jacob Webber, William Nelles, Johannis Kisler, Geo. Breigel, Joh. Schaffer, Geo. Dachstader, Johannes Zaysdorf.

"*From Haybury:* John Christopher Fucks, John Wm. Daies, John Wm. Schaff, Christian Bauch, Peter Hayd, Henr. Hammer, Mich. Ittich, Johan. Kyser,

Jacob Cup, Paulus Dientzer, Melch. Foltz, John Segendorf, Philip Laux, Abraham Langen, Jno. Jacob Schultz, Joh. Wm. Hambuch, Niclaus Laux, Niclaus Gottel, Paulus Reitchoff.

"*From Annesburg:* Hartmann Weindecker, Captain. Joh. Wm. Dill, Peter Speis, Herman Bitzer, Johannes Schue, John Wm. Schneider, Jacob Bast, Johannes Blass, Johann Wm. Kammer, Joh. Bonroth, Johannes Benhard, Sebastian Fischer, Niclaus Hayd, Henrick Klein, Ben. Balt. Stuper, Casper Rauch, Hans Hen. Zeller, Johannes Zeller, Samuel Kuhn, Gerhard Schaffer, Ulrich Bruckhart, Jacob Ess, Ferdo. Mentegen, Conrad Kuhn, Valtin Kuhn, Henrich Winter, Joh. Geo. Reiffenberg, John Wm. Linck, Jno. Martin Netzbach, Johannes Weis, Jno. Adam Walbourn, Jno. Henry Arendorf, Danl. Busch, Jno. Henry Conradt, Hen. Bellinger, Johan Schneider, Marcus Bellinger, Phil. Schaffer, Johan. Kradt, Christ. Sittenich, Jno. Henry Schmidt, Jno. Philipl Zerbe, Niclaus Ruhl, Adam Mic. Schmidt, Conrad Maisinger, Thos. Ruffener, Jacob Dings, Henrick Fehling, Joh. Jost Petry, Lud. W. Schmidt.

"*From Hunterstown:* Jno. Peter Kneskern, Captain. David Huppert, Conrad Schawerman, Henrick Sex, Frederick Bell, Jacob Kobell, Jacob Warno, Johannes Schulteis, Reinhard Schaffer, Johannes Roschman, Garl Uhl, Baltz Anspach, Conrad Keller, Jno. George Schmidt, Conrad Goldman, Geo. Bender, Jno. Henry Uhl, Tho. Schumacher, Peter Schmidt, Johan. Schwall, Geo. Ludwig Koch, Veil Musig, Gro. Keschner, Chris. Hills, Rudol. Stahl.

These lists are composed entirely of residents of the villages on the east side of the Hudson. There must have been troops also from the three villages on the west side.

But the confidence of the Governor was not won by this service, and when the campaign was over they were disarmed, under the apprehension that they might turn their arms against the province. "They have since used some artifices," writes the Governor, "and made some false alarms in order to induce me to restore their arms; but to no purpose. They are planted where they are covered every way." A regiment of troops is asked for to garrison the country in the neighborhood of the Palatines, to keep them to their duty. With nothing to encourage them in their labor, we can readily appreciate Hunter's complaint that, except by resorting to force, it was hard to keep them at work. When, however, he adopted a more conciliatory method, and offered them one-half of the proceeds, the expedient proved successful. But the Governor was impoverished, and was at last compelled to inform them that, during the winter of 1712–13, they must rely upon their own resources for support. "I had no remedy left," he writes, "but to intimate to that people, that they should take measures to subsist themselves during this winter upon

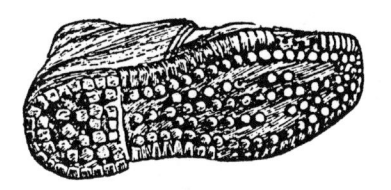

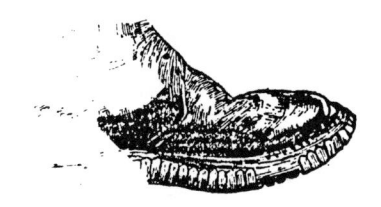

Relics of the Palatines in New York.

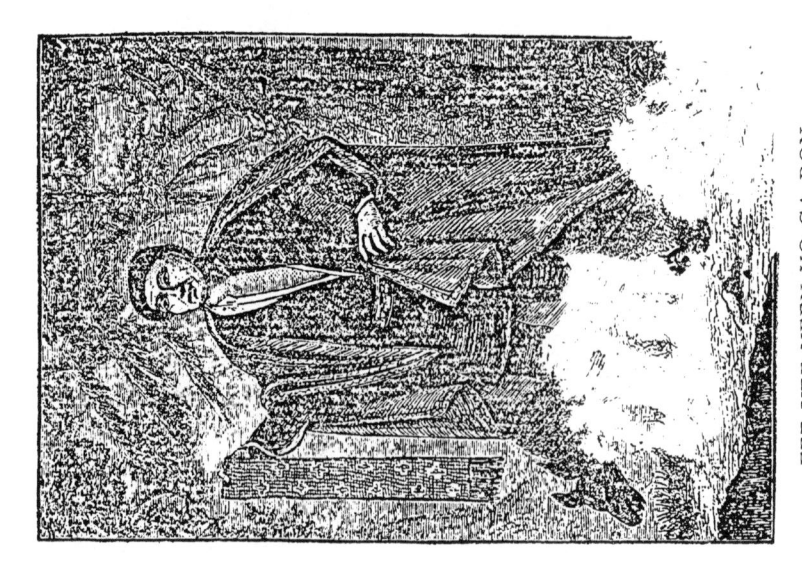

FEE YEE NEEN IIO GA RON,
Emperor of the Six Nations.

SA GA YEATH QUA PIETH TON,
King of the Maquas.

the lands where they were planted, and such as could not, might find it by working with the inhabitants, leaving with the commissaries their names and the names of the places or landlords where they are employed during that time, that they may be in readiness upon the first public notice, given, to return to work."

Thus the contract was broken on the side of the Governor. The tidings struck consternation into the Palatines. Winter was just at hand. Starvation was imminent. Something had to be done at once, or they were lost. Thrown upon their own resources, the more enterprising among them proceeded to provide for themselves in a way Hunter had not anticipated. True to the German instinct to go to first sources, they determined, without the intervention of any third party, like Livingstone, to deal directly with the first proprietors of the soil, the Indians. They recalled the fact that several Indian chiefs, who had visited England, while they were encamped in London, had presented Queen Anne with a tract of ground, near Schoharie, for their use. A delegation headed by the elder Weiser was sent accordingly to the Indians to state their extremity, and to ask permission for them to settle on the lands that had been donated. The Indians acted in good faith. In less than two weeks after the return of the delegation, fifty families moved to Schoharie, by way of Schenectady, constructing over a portion of the way fifteen miles of roadway through the forests. Reaching their destination they found a prohibition from the Governor awaiting them, accompanied with the threat that, unless

ECON OH KOAN,
King of the River Nation.

HO NEE YEATH TAN NO RON,
King of the Generechgarich.

they would return they would be treated as rebels. No alternative was in their power but to remain and take the consequences. In March, 1713, they were followed by a large number of their kindred, who broke their way through three feet of snow. More ground was needed for their support than the Indians had donated. Certain citizens of Albany prompted by their antipathy towards Germans, cherished at the time by the Dutch settlers and their descendants, sought to preëmpt the land; but, favored by the friendship of the Indians, all that they needed was procured for three hundred dollars. From the Indians they learned the use of certain roots (probably potatoes) and wild herbs (as beans, etc.), and where to look for them. They refer to the fact that what was said to Adam in wrath: "Of the grass of the field thou shalt eat," was said to them in grace.

To the Board of Trade, Hunter explained that he had been powerless to prevent this movement. He consoled himself with the assurance, that, while, without his license, they could obtain no title to the land, they would prove, if successful, a good protection for the frontier, and a new field would be opened for the manufacture of tar.

It was to a beautiful and fertile country that they were thus strangely led. Twenty thousand acres came into their possession. The people, numbering from five to seven hundred, were settled in seven villages, named after the deputies who had treated with the Indians, and who had then led the colony to Schoharie, viz., Kneskerndorf, Gerlachsdorf, Fuchsendorf, Schmidtsdorf, Weisersdorf,

Hartmansdorf and Ober Weisersdorf. Four children, William Bouck, Catharine Mattice, Elizabeth Sawyer and John Earhart were born the week after their arrival. They were without a pastor, but a tailor wrote to Boehme that he was acting as a lay preacher.

Upon the history of Schoharie, whose details have been well preserved, both in contemporary documents, and by industrious collectors of traditions many years ago, we cannot linger. When we consider that the Palatines carried with them none of the agricultural implements with which they had been furnished on the Hudson; that, in the beginning, there was not even a wheelbarrow in the colony, much less a horse or a cow, the progress made with the most primitive appliances for tilling the soil was most surprising. A vivid picture of the hardships of their primitive mode of life has been drawn by a local authority: "For several years they had most of their grain floured at Schenectady. They usually went in parties of fifteen or twenty at a time, to be able to defend themselves against the wild beasts. Often there were as many women as men on these journeys, and as they had to encamp in the woods at least one night, the women frequently displayed, when in danger, as much courage as their liege lords. A skipple was the quantity usually borne by each individual, but the stronger often carried more. Not infrequently they left Schoharie to go to mill on the morning of one day, and were at home on the morning of the next; performing a journey of between forty and fifty miles in twenty-four hours or less, bearing the ordinary burden; but at such

THE PENNSYLVANIA-GERMAN SOCIETY.

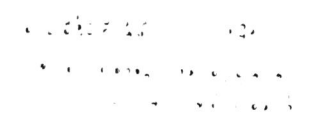

WILLIAM C. BOUCK,

B. 1786; D. 1859.

GOVERNOR OF NEW YORK, 1843-45, NAMESAKE AND DESCENDANT OF WILLIAM BOUCK,
WHO WAS BORN DURING THE FIRST WEEK OF THE SCHOHARIE SETTLEMENT.

times, they traveled most of the night without encamping." [1]

The Palatines owed much to the continued friendly relations of the Indians. One proof is given in the fact that, during the first winter, John Conrad Weiser sent his son Conrad to live among the Mohawks and learn their language. But while the Indians were conciliated, their Dutch neighbors seemed to them merciless. Looking back, as we may now do, we must concede that there were faults on both sides. Our ancestors and kinsmen in their ignorance of the processes of law, and with a deep sense of injustice, undoubtedly forfeited some of their rights, but could not be persuaded that they were wrong. They claimed the absolute right to lands which the Indians had given or sold them, and first ignored, and then resisted every attempt of the Provincial authorities to establish the titles. When Nicholas Bayard was sent to give them deeds in the name of the Crown, upon the simple condition that each householder show the boundaries of the lands that he had taken, he was driven off under a hot fire of bullets. From Schoharie, he offered a deed to every one who would bring in payment a single ear of corn; but this offer no one accepted. In November, 1714, therefore, the lands were sold to certain Dutch citizens of Albany. The Palatines found that attempts were made to turn the Indians against them. But this was recognized as a very dangerous expedient, since Weiser's influence with the Mohawks could not be overcome. Every effort made by the

---

[1] *History of Schoharie County and Border Wars of New York*, by J. W. Simms, Albany, 1845.

purchasers to settle on the lands was resisted. An interesting report is that of Adam Vrooman to the Governor concerning the ground that he had sowed with grain, upon which the Palatines drove their horses by night; and the house that he had well under way, which he found one morning razed to the ground, the Palatines concealing their operations by driving horses with bells upon them all through the night. "John Conrad Weiser," he continues, "has been the ringleader of all factions; for he has had his son sometime to live among the Indians, and now he is turned their interpreter; so that this Weiser and his son talk with the Indians very often, and have made treaties for them, and have been busy to buy land at many places."[1] The charge was afterwards made by Hunter in Weiser's presence, before the Board of Trade in England, that he had brought down the Indians of The Five Nations upon the Dutch grantees.

Sheriff Adams was finally sent down from Albany to assert the supremacy of the law, and arrest Weiser. When he reached Weisersdorf, now Middleburg, Schoharie Co., the Palatine women took the responsibility of a defence from the shoulders of their husbands and fathers, and, under the leadership of Margeret Zeh, knocked him down, rolled him in the mud, and lifting him on a rail, carried him the distance of six or seven miles, and left him on a log bridge on the road to Albany. He returned a thoroughly bruised and humiliated man, with two broken ribs, and the loss of an eye. We must commend the for-

---

[1] *Documentary History of New York*, III., 412.

bearance of the Governor, in attempting no immediate arrests for this flagrant violation of the law. But unsuspecting members of the settlements who went to Albany on business, were arrested and imprisoned. That Weiser came to intimidate the Governor, with three or four hundred armed men, we know only from Hunter's testimony in Weiser's presence in 1720. In order to end the struggle, the Governor finally summoned their representatives to Albany in 1717, and informed them that, unless they purchased the ground they would be transported to another place, and their improvements paid for at an appraised value by the Province.

There seemed to be but one remedy; and that was to appeal to the Board of Trade through personal representatives. On this errand, Weiser, Scheff and Walrath were secretly sent in 1718. Captured by pirates in Delaware Bay, they were robbed, and Weiser thrice tied up and cruelly beaten. After a long delay reaching England, Pastor Boehme's influence at length secured for them a hearing before the Board; but not until they had been imprisoned for debt, and Walrath had started for home and died. The following is the petition of Scheff and Weiser:

"That, in the year 1709, the Palatines and other Germans, being invited to come into England about four thousand of them were sent to New York in America, of whom about 1700 died on board, or at their landing in that Province by unavoidable sickness.

"That before they went on board they were promised, those remaining alive should have forty acres of land and five pounds sterling a head, besides clothes, tools, utensils and other necessaries to husbandry to be given on their arrival in America.

"That on their landing they were quartered in tents, and divided into six companies, having each a captain of their own nation, with a promise of an allowance of fifteen pounds per annum to each commander.

"That afterwards they were removed on lands belonging to Mr. Livingstone, where they erected small houses for shelter during the winter seasons.

"That in the Spring following they were ordered into the woods to make pitch and tar, where they lived about two years; but the country not being fit to raise any considerable quantity of naval stores, they were commanded to build, to clear and improve the ground belonging to a private person.

"That the Indians having yielded to Her late Majesty of pious memory a small tract of land called Schorie for the use of the Palatines, they, in fifteen days, cleared a way of fifteen miles through the woods, and settled fifty families therein.

"That in the following Spring the remainder of the said Palatines joined the said fifty families so settled therein Schorie.

"But that country being too small for their increasing families, they were constrained to purchase some neighboring land of the Indians, for which they were to give three hundred pieces of eight.

"And having built small houses and huts, there about one year after the said purchase some gentlemen of Albany, declared to the Palatines, that themselves having purchased the said country of Schorie of the Governor of New York, they would not permit them to live there, unless an agreement was also made with those of Albany; but that the Palatines having refused to enter into such agreement, a sheriff and some officers were sent from Albany to seize one of their captains, who being upon his guard, the Indians were animated against the Palatines; but these found means to appease the savages by giving them what they would of their own substance.

"That in the year 1717 the Governor of New York having summoned the Palatines to appear at Albany, some of them being deputed went accordingly, where they were told that unless they did agree with the gentlemen of Albany, the Governor expected an order from England to transport them to another place, and that he would send twelve men to view their works and improvements to appraise the same, and then to give them the value thereof in money.

"But this not being done, the Palatines, to the number of about three thousand, have continued to manure and sow the land, that they might not be starved for want of corn and food.

"For which manuring the gentlemen of Albany have put in prison one man and one woman, and will not release them, unless they have sufficient security of One Hundred Crowns for the former.

"Now in order that the Palatines may be preserved in the Land of Schorie, which they have purchased of the Indians, or that they may be so settled in an adjoining tract of land, as to raise a necessary subsistence for themselves and their families, they have sent into England three persons, one of whom is since dead, humbly to lay their case before His Majesty, not doubting but that in consideration of the hardships they have suffered for want of a secure settlement,

His Majesty's ministers and Councils will compassionate those His faithful subjects.

"Who, in the first year after their arrival willingly and cheerfully sent three hundred men to the expedition against Canada, and afterwards to the assistance of Albany which was threatened by the French and Indians, for which service they never received one penny, tho' they were upon the establishment of New York or New Jersey; nor had they received one penny of the five pounds per head promised at their going on board from England; neither have their commanders received anything of the allowance of fifteen pounds per annum; and though the arms they had given them at the Canada expedition, which were, by special order of Her late Majesty, to be left in their possession, have been taken from them, yet they are still ready to fight against all the enemies of His Majesty and those countries, whenever there shall be occasion to show their hearty endeavor for the prosperity of their generous benefactors in England, as well as in America.

"Therefore, they hope from the justice of the Right Honorable Lords Commissioners of Trade and Plantations, to whom their petition to their excellencies the Lord Justices has been referred, that they shall be so supported by their Lordships' report, as to be represented fit objects to be secured in the land they now do inhabit, or in some near adjoining lands remaining in the right of the Crown in the said Province of New York."[1] August 2, 1720.

But a new difficulty arose. The far-seeing eye of Weiser had Pennsylvania in view as the proper home of his

---

[1] *Documents relating to the Colonial History of New York*, V., 553-5.

THE PENNSYLVANIA-GERMAN SOCIETY.

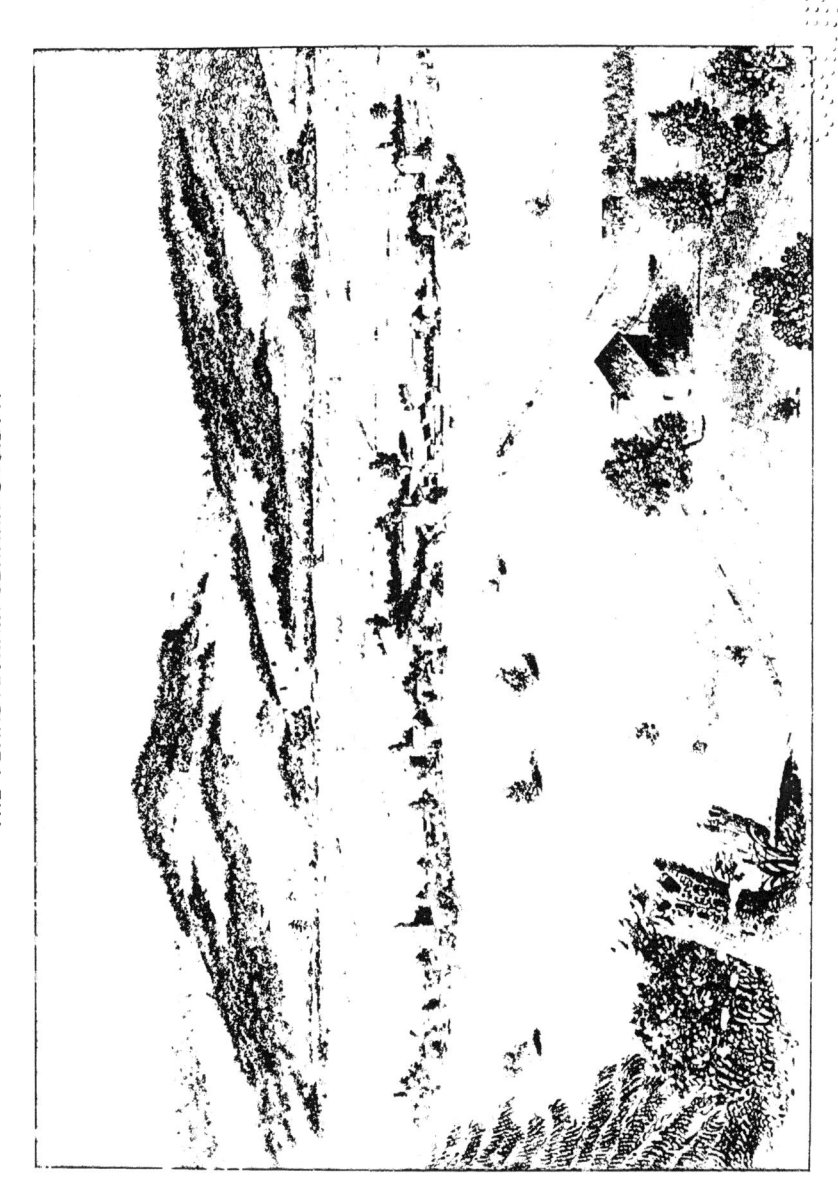

THE VALLEY OF SCHOHARIE

people. He conceived the scheme of securing from the government an exchange of their lands in New York for others on the Swatara. To this Scheff was violently opposed, and accordingly filed his protest with the Board, declaring any such proposition of Weiser a violation of instructions. "Your petitioner," he writes, "hearing with grief that John Conrad Weiser has petitioned your Lordships, for obtaining a tract of land called Chettery [Swatara], most humbly entreats your Lordships to dismiss the said Weiser's petition as being directly contrary to our instructions and the inclinations of our people, who earnestly desire to lead a quiet and peaceable life, and are utterly averse to expose their tender children and child-bearing women to another transportation by water, as still remembering the loss of most of their young children at their going from home to America."[1]

Hunter's recall to England and his appearance before the Board was an effectual obstacle to any efforts for the confirmation of their titles to their lands. Lands in other localities in New York were offered instead to those willing to remove. Some, accepting this offer, removed to the district known as Stony Arabia. Others, who, by their thrift, had accumulated means, purchased their old homes. But still others, chiefly from Hartmansdorf and Weisersdorf followed Weiser's advice, as the best solution of the problem, and turned their faces southward towards Pennsylvania.

As we turn from New York to descend the Susquehanna with these pioneers, we may interrupt the narrative for a

[1] *Documents relating to the Colonial History of New York*, V., 575.

few moments, and, going forward nearly a quarter of a century, look upon the closing scene of the life of their leader, as it shows whence his intrepid courage and undaunted perseverance came.

"In the year 1746," writes Henry Melchior Muhlenberg, " my wife's grandfather, Conrad Weiser, Sr., came to my house, having been living in the Province of New York, since 1710, and more recently on the borders of New England. * * * He was so much exhausted by the long and fatiguing journey at his great age, that he was almost dead when he was brought into my house. After he had been resting in bed for twenty-four hours, and had partaken of some nourishment he was refreshed. Then he began in half broken accents, devoutly to repeat the hymn: '*Schwing dich auf zu deinem Gott,*' etc., especially repeating the third verse. His eyesight was very dim; his hearing was so dull that I could not speak much with him; but as I listened to him repeating from his heart passages of Scripture, such as: 'Surely He hath borne our griefs,' etc., 'This is a faithful saying and worthy of all acceptation,' etc., 'God was in Christ reconciling the world unto Himself,' etc., 'For God so loved the world,' etc., I could not refrain from tears of joy. To these he added verses concerning the personal appropriation of Christ, as 'Come unto me all ye that labor,' etc., 'Him that cometh unto me I will in no wise cast out,' etc., ' Father, I have sinned against Heaven,' etc., and ' God, be merciful to me a sinner.' He repeated also '*Ach vater deck all meine Suende,*' the sixth stanza of the hymn, '*Wer weiss wie nahe mir mein Ende.*'

> ' O Father, cover all my sins
>   With Jesus' merits, Who alone
>   The pardon that I covet wins,
>   And make His long-sought rest my own.
> My God, for Jesus' sake I pray,
> Thy peace may bless my dying day.'[1]

"I had everything quieted around him, so that he might not notice the presence of any one, in order that he might alone and in spirit hold communion with the Omipresent God. * * * He expressed an anxious desire for the Holy Supper, adding that as there had been no pastors in the region where he had been living he had not received it for some years. It was Sunday, and some members of our congregation had called before the hour of worship. So he made confession of his sins, humbled himself in the presence of his Saviour, as a poor worm, worthy of condemnation, implored grace and pardon, and asked for the Holy Spirit, that he might lead a better life. Such an impression was made on all present that they were melted to tears. * * * In the meantime my father-in-law sent a wagon for him, furnished with a bed, and so had him conveyed to his own home, fifty miles up the country. Upon leaving, he gave us his blessing. He arrived at the house of his son, after a very fatiguing journey, and lived yet for a short time with his Joseph in Goshen. Then, at last, he fell asleep amid the loving prayers and sighs of his children and his childrens' children, who stood around him, his wandering in his pilgrimage having been continued between eighty and ninety years."[2]

---

[1] Translation of Miss Winkworth.

[2] *Hallesche Nachrichten*, old ed., pp. 161–3; *Lutheran Church Review*, XI., 391–4.

CHAPTER VI.—TO PENNSYLVANIA.

Arms of Pennsylvania from contemporary print.

IN 1723 under the guidance of the Indians a road was cut from the Schoharie to the Susquehanna. Over this thirty-three families transported their goods. Canoes and rafts were built, and the most of the people were thus carried to their new home, while the cattle were driven along the bank. Down the Susquehanna they went to the mouth of the Swatara, up the Swatara, to the Tulpehocken, and thence settlements were formed along that creek. Thus they become pioneers of portions of Dauphin, Lebanon and Berks counties. A tradition current in the Schoharie settlement, which may be given for what it is worth, states that twelve of the horses of the Tulpehocken colony not approving the

THE PENNSYLVANIA-GERMAN SOCIETY.

change, broke loose, twelve of them arriving in good condition at Schoharie a year and a half after their removal, having completed a journey of over three hundred miles! A partial list of the Schoharie immigrants to the Tulpehocken region has been included by Mr. Rupp in Appendix XIV. of his invaluable book. Five years later, they were followed by others. The younger Weiser states that the settlement was made in Pennsylvania without the consent of the Proprietary of Pennsylvania or his commissionaries, and against the consent of the Indians. For a considerable time, they were absolutely without any law or government. The older Weiser did not accompany the expedition he had projected; the younger removed to Tulpehocken from Schoharie in 1729. The preceding year, fifteen heads of families had petitioned for the right of purchasing land, stating that fifty other families were in the same circumstances, and desired the same privilege.[1]

Meanwhile during all these years the emigration to Pennsylvania had proceeded, notwithstanding the diversion to the Carolinas and New York. The cruel diversion of a large number of Germans to Louisiana in 1716 in connection with the so-called Mississippi bubble of John Law and the death of the vast majority was an episode that only made Pennsylvania more popular. The Palatines spread the story of their wrongs far and wide among their kinsmen in Germany, and turned the tide whither it had been first directed by the efforts and invitations of Penn. Peter Kalm, the Swedish naturalist, who visited this country in

[1] *Colonial Records of Pennsylvania*, III., p. 323.

En Resa til Norra AMERICA,

På Kongl. Swenska Wetenskaps Academiens befallning, Och Publict kostnad, Förrättad Af

PEHR KALM,

Oeconomiæ Professor i Åbo, samt Ledamot af Kongl. Swenska Wetenskaps-Academien.

Tom. II.

Med Kongl. Maj:ts Allernådigste Privilegio.

STOCKHOLM,
Tryckt på LARS SALVII kostnad, 1756.

Title of Kalm's *Travels in North America*.

1748, writes: "The Germans wrote to their relatives and friends, and advised them, if ever they intended to come to America, not to go to New York, where the Government had shown itself to be inequitable. This advice had so much influence that the Germans who afterwards went in great numbers to North America, constantly avoided New York, and always went to Pennsylvania. It sometimes happened that they were forced to go on board such ships as were bound for New York, but they were scarcely got on shore, before they hastened to Pennsylvania, in sight of all the inhabitants of New York."[1]

The efforts of Kocherthal had only temporarily diverted or retarded the main stream of German emigration to Pennsylvania. It now flowed on in a strong and steady current, gathering around the nucleus formed by the Frankford Land Company, thence diffusing itself throughout the southeastern corner of the province, and after crossing the Susquehanna, sending its overflow into Maryland and the Shenandoah Valley of Virginia. The details of this immigration are outside the limits of the present paper, which, according to the assignment, is simply to bring the emigrants to our borders, and leave them there, for other writers to complete the work. A few facts, however, are in place.

Pennsylvania, we believe, became a favorite of German emigrants because of the religious principles embodied in its laws. These were, first the clear recognition of Christianity as the basis of the government, and, secondly, the

---
[1] *Travels in America*, I., p. 270 sq.

toleration granted, within certain limits for various forms of Christianity. The fact that the German emigration proceeded in clearly-marked waves, according to diverse denominations and sects, beginning with those most persecuted in Europe, and thence proceeding to those where the religious restraints in the mother country were more a matter of annoyance than of persecution, supports this opinion. "The History of Religious Liberty in Pennsylvania" would be a fruitful theme for an entire paper.

Penn, in the preface to his *Frame of Laws*, bases all civil government upon Divine authority as proclaimed in the Holy Scriptures, and lays down principles in axiomatic form that are worthy of lasting memory. "Let men be good, and the government cannot be bad; if it be ill, they will cure it. But if men be bad, let the government be never so good, they will endeavor to warp and spoil it to their turn." The very first law contained in the Petition of Rights of 1682 makes it one of the qualifications of members of the Assembly and of those who have the right to vote for members, that they "shall be such as profess and declare that they believe in Jesus Christ to be the Son of God, the Saviour of the world."[1] Among the laws agreed upon in England in 1682, and in force in 1682-1700, is the following: "That all persons living in this province, who confess and acknowledge the One Almighty and Eternal God to be the Creator, Upholder and Ruler of the world, and that hold themselves obliged in conscience to live peaceably and justly in civil society,

---
[1] *Duke of York's Laws*, etc., Harrisburg, 1879, p. 19 sq.

shall in no ways be molested or prejudiced for their religious persuasion or practice in matters of faith and worship, nor shall they be compelled at any time to frequent or maintain any religious worship, place or ministry whatever."[1] In 1697, this law was reënacted, with the additional clause: "and if any person shall abuse or deride any other for his or her different persuasion or practice in matter of religion, such person shall be looked upon as a disturber of the peace and be punished accordingly." This was afterwards declared by enactment to be the very first of the Fundamental Laws of the Province.[2] When again enacted in 1700, it was repealed by the Queen in Council upon the exception of the Attorney-General—"I am of the opinion that this law is not fit to be confirmed, no regard being had in it to the Christian religion, and also for that in the indulgence allowed to the Quakers in England, by the statute of the first by William and Mary, chapt. 18 (which sort of people are also the principal inhabitants of Pennsylvania) they are obliged by the declaration to profess faith in God, and in Jesus Christ, His Eternal Son, the True God, and in the Holy Spirit, One God Blessed forevermore; and to acknowledge the Scriptures of the Old and New Testaments to be given by Divine inspiration, and also for that none can tell for what conscientious practices allowed by this act may extend to."[3]

In accordance, therefore, with these exceptions of the Attorney-General, there resulted the Act of 1705–6, which

---
[1] *Duke of York's Laws*, etc., p. 102 sq. [2] Ib., p. 154.
[3] *Statutes at Large for Pennsylvania*, 1682–1800. Compiled by James F. Mitchell and Henry Flanders, II., 489.

was in force during the entire period embraced in this paper. The recognition of the Trinity and of the inspiration of the Holy Scriptures was in no way objectionable to the great body of the German immigrants, while the liberty offered from the restraints of ecclesiasticism was particularly appreciated not merely by those who were generally regarded as "sects," but by the adherents also of the Pietistic movement. The Act is as follows:

"Almighty God, being only Lord of conscience, author of all divine knowledge, faith and worship, who can only enlighten the minds and convince the understanding of people; in due reverence to His sovereignty over the souls of mankind, and the better to unite the Queen's subjects in interest and affection; Be it enacted, that no person now or at any time hereafter dwelling or residing within this province, who shall profess faith in God the Father, and in Jesus Christ His only Son, and in the Holy Spirit, One God blessed forevermore, and shall acknowledge the Holy Scriptures of the Old and New Testaments to be given by divine inspiration, and when lawfully required shall profess and declare that they will live peaceably under the constituted government, shall, in any case, be molested or prejudiced for his or her conscience persuasion, nor shall he or she be at any time compelled to frequent or maintain any religious worship, place or ministry whatever, contrary to his or her mind, but shall freely and fully enjoy his or her Christian liberty in all respects, without molestation or interruption."[1]

---

[1] Acts of the General Assembly of Pennsylvania at session October 14, 1705–February 12, 1706. *Laws of the Commonwealth of Pennsylvania,* 1700-1810, I, p. 94.

Among the movements which may be ascribed to these laws guaranteeing liberty of conscience, was the Mennonite emigration to the Pequea District in Lancaster County, between 1709 and 1717—a branch from the Germantown settlement forming the beginning, which was greatly reinforced by recruits from Switzerland and Germany secured through the mission to Europe of Martin Kendig. Dunkards and other Mennonites are said to have reached Lehigh County not much later. Even before this (1704-12), before and contemporaneously with the Palatine emigration to New York, other of their countrymen, mostly Reformed and Lutheran, can be traced filling up the Oley region, with its center in Berks, although standing in the old records for a much more extensive territory than the township of that name. So also the District in Montgomery County about the headwaters of the Perkiomen was settled by the same people before the Palatines descended the Susquehanna. The Allens and Wisters and other land speculators in Philadelphia had found customers among those who arrived at the port, and had sold them homes in Northampton. The Palatines from New York at Tulpehocken and Quitapahilla had attracted to this country many of their relatives and friends whom they had left in Germany.

No more vivid picture could be drawn of the condition of the majority of the emigrants than a letter of Casper Wistar, already referred to. We quote from the "*Sammlung auserlesener Materien zum Bau des Reichs Gottes*" (Leipzig), for 1733, where it is credited to the Leipzig

"*Zeitungen*" of May 22, 1733, having been written in Philadelphia, November 8, 1732.

"Being importuned daily by so many of our countrymen to relieve them from the great distress, into which they have come, partially through their own thoughtlessness, and partially by the persuasion of others, and it being absolutely impossible to help all, sympathy for the poor people still in the Fatherland, and who, before undertaking such a journey, have time to reflect, constrains me to give a true account of the condition of things in this new land. I make this particular request that these facts may be reported everywhere, that no one may have the excuse for learning them only from his own personal experience.

"Some years ago this was a very fruitful country, and, like all new countries, but sparsely inhabited. Since the wilderness required much labor, and the inhabitants were few, ships that arrived with German emigrants were cordially welcomed. They were immediately discharged, and by their labor very easily earned enough to buy some land. Pennsylvania is but a small part of America, and has been open now for some years, so that not only many thousand Germans, but English and Irish have settled there, and filled all parts of the country; so that all who now seek land must go far into the wilderness, and purchase it at a higher price.

"Many hardships also are experienced on the voyage. Last year one of the ships was driven about the ocean for twenty-four weeks, and of its one hundred and fifty passengers, more than one hundred starved to death. To satisfy their hunger, they caught mice and rats; and a mouse brought half a gulden. When the survivors at last reached land, their sufferings were aggravated by their arrest, and the exaction from them of the entire fare for both living and dead. This year ten ships with three thousand souls have arrived.

"One of these vessels was seventeen weeks on the way and about sixty of its passengers died at sea. All the survivors are sick and feeble, and, what is worst, poor and without means; hence, in a community like this where money is scarce, they are a burden, and every day there are deaths among them. Every person over fourteen years old, must pay six doubloons (about 90 dollars) passage from Rotterdam, and those between four and fourteen must pay half that amount. When one is without the money, his only resource is to sell himself for a term of from three to eight years or more, and to serve as a slave. Nothing but a poor suit of clothes is received when his time has expired. Families endure a great trial when they see the father purchased by one master, the mother by another, and each of the children by another. All this for the money only that they owe the Captain. And yet they are only too glad, when after waiting long, they at last find some one willing to buy them; for the money of the country is well nigh exhausted. In view of these circumstances, and the tedious, expensive and perilous voyage, you should not advise any one for whom you wish well to come hither. All I can say is that those who think of coming should weigh well what has been above stated, and should count the cost, and, above all, should go to God for counsel and inquire whether it be His will, lest they may undertake that whereof they will afterward repent. If ready to hazard their lives and to endure patiently all the trials of the voyage, they must farther think whether over and above the cost they will have enough to purchase cattle, and to provide for other necessities. No one should rely upon friends whom he may have here; for they have enough to do, and many a one reckons in this without his host. Young and able-bodied persons, who can do efficient work, can, nevertheless, always find some one who will purchase them for two, three or four years; but they must be unmarried. For young married persons, particularly when the wife is with child, no one cares to have. So also with old people and children. Of mechanics there are a considerable number already here; but a good mechanic who can bring with him sufficient capital to avoid beginning with debt, may do well, although of almost all classes and occupations, there are already more than too many. All this I have, out of sincere love for the interests of my neighbor, deemed it necessary to communicate concerning the present condition in Pennsylvania. With this I commit my beloved friend to the protection of God, and always remain

"His sincere friend,

"CASPAR WISTAR."

But it is a mistake to suppose that these emigrants were always impoverished. They often brought with them a modest capital with which to begin life on this side of the ocean. Some were in good circumstances and were able to buy large farms. Their usual course was from Germany to Rotterdam in Holland, thence to England, and thence to Philadelphia. "The frequency with which the same craft, as shown by the records, entered the capes of the Delaware, implied a traffic partaking somewhat of the character of a ferry. For year after year the ships *St. Andrew*, *Phœnix*, *Dragon*, *Patience*, *Mortonhouse*, *Pennsylvania*, *The Two Brothers*, *Nancy* and many others discharged their human cargoes at Philadelphia, the average passenger lists embracing one hundred and fifty souls. In the year 1719 some six thousand are said to have landed, in 1732 ten vessels with three thousand passengers, and Proud avers that in the year 1749 twelve thousand Germans arrived in the Province. Sypher claims that prior to 1727 fifty thousand people, mostly from the Rhine country, had emigrated to the Quaker colony."[1] At the middle of the century the German population of Pennsylvania was about one-half of the whole. Not until 1717 was any record of passengers kept, but as the stream began to flow in large mass the wise precaution of Lieut.-Governor Keith, requiring all immigrants to take the oath of allegiance and be registered in Philadelphia, furnished the historical data which the late Mr. I. D. Rupp has industriously gathered and embodied in his valuable Thirty Thousand Names. These lists of male immigrants over sixteen years of age began in 1727. It is possible they are incomplete, as there are gaps that may, and yet may not be explained, since these vessels all arrived at the same period of the year. Thus there are no records between October, 1727, and August, 1728; September, 1728, and August,

---

[1] A. D. Melick, Jr., *The Pennsylvania Magazine of History and Biography*, X., 391.

1729, September, 1729, and August, 1730. In the last three weeks of 1732 no less than 1,500 people arrived, while in August and September, 1733, 1,369 are reported.

The Lutheran pastors, Muhlenberg, Brunnholtz and Handschuh, in reporting the religious condition of the German immigrants to Halle, in 1754, divide the history of the immigration into five periods. The first was from 1680 to 1708; the second, from 1708 to 1720. Of the latter, they say: "In the years 1708, 1709, 1710 to 1720, when there was a great movement from the Palatinate to England, and a large number of people were sent thence to New York, under Queen Anne, not a few came from the same source to Pennsylvania also." They were largely people of a religious character, and brought with them Arndt's *True Christianity* and volumes of sermons and Prayer Books, besides the ponderous Bibles so familiar to their descendants among the heirlooms of their fathers; but, according to this report, their neglect to provide for themselves churches and ministers bore bitter fruit in the relative religious indifference of the next generation. Towards the close of the same period, they note the arrival of members of such communities as the Tunkers, Mennonites, Schwenckfelders, etc., of whom we have more accurate information elsewhere. The third period is from 1720 to 1730, with a large immigration from the Palatinate, Würtemberg, Hesse-Darmstadt and other districts, as well as of many of the New York Palatines. Among them, there seemed more religious earnestness; but their extreme poverty prevented them from securing sufficient pastors. At the close of this period and the beginning of the next, from 1730 to 1740, a still more extensive immigration followed. This immigration moved in successive waves, representing different religious denominations.

Peter Tranberg
Pastor in Willmington

Henry Melchior Muhlenberg
minister at Providence and Newhanover.

Gabr. Naesman Minister
at ye Swedes Church at Wicaco.

Peter Brunnholtz,
minister at Philadelphia
(and Germantown).

Signatures of the German Lutheran pastors, Muhlenberg and Brunnholtz, with those of their Swedish associates at Wilmington, and Gloria Dei Church, Philadelphia.

With some marked exceptions, it may be said that the communities composed of separatists from the State Churches came first; then came the Reformed; then the Lutherans; then the Moravians. The Reformed pastor Weiss reports in 1731 no less than 15,000 members of his Church in Pennsylvania. Twenty years later Rev. Michael Schlatter estimated the entire population as 190,000, of whom 90,000 were Germans and 30,000 Reformed. Dr. J. H. Dubbs claims that up to the middle of the last century, the Reformed were by far the most numerous religious body in the Province. The Reformed Classis of Amsterdam in 1751, wrote that Pennsylvania was probably a Pella or Zoar, whence the godly might escape from the calamities threatening the Old World, and add that thousands of immigrants, chiefly from the Palatinate and Switzerland, and the majority of them adherents to the Reformed faith, have already taken refuge there.[1]

Welcomed at first, and their labor in advancing the general prosperity recognized, the extent of the immigration began as early as 1717 to occasion apprehension on the part of the English settlers, which increased to positive hostility, as years brought no cessation of the stream. In 1728, Governor Thomas estimated the Germans as constituting three-fifths of the entire population. The words of Benjamin Franklin in 1751 may be recalled as a proof of the vastness of the movement: "Why should the Palatine boors be suffered to swarm into our settlements, and, by herding together, establish their language and manners, to

---
[1] Fresenius. *Pastoral-Sammlung*, XII., 219.

the exclusion of ours? Why should Pennsylvania, founded by the English, become a colony of aliens, who will shortly be so numerous as to Germanize us, instead of our Anglicifying them, and will never adopt our language or customs any more than they can acquire our complexion?" Dr. William Smith, the Provost of the University of Pennsylvania, thought it possible that the Provincial Legislature would be forced to appoint an official interpreter, that one-half of the legislators might be able to understand the other half, and to save Pennsylvania from the threatened heathenism, organized a "*Society for the Propagation of the Gospel among the Germans!*" Alarmists were constantly raising the cry of an imminent peril of an alliance between the Pennsylvania Germans and the French, on the west, that would be fatal to English dominance. Franklin was soon made to feel that he had committed a political blunder by his strongly expressed hostility to the immigrants, and tried to explain that the term "boor," he had employed, was only a synonym for "farmer;" while he freely conceded the important contribution they made to the development of Pennsylvania. "Their industry and frugality are exemplary. They are excellent husbandmen and contribute greatly to the improvement of a country." In 1738, the Governor, in a message to the Provincial Assembly, had declared: "This Province has been for some time the asylum of the distressed Protestants of the Palatinate, and other parts of Germany; and I believe it may with truth be said that the present flourishing condition of it is in great measure owing to the industry of those people." [1]

When in 1729, Thomas Mackin, the Principal of the Philadelphia Academy, undertook to celebrate the growing prosperity of the Province, he both alludes to the numbers and the importance of our fathers in the words:

> " Twas hither first the British crossed the main;
> Thence many others left their native plain;
> Hibernia's sons forsake their native home;
> And from Germania, crowded vessels come.
> Not for themselves alone the British care;
> Since every stranger may partake a share.
> Hence still more culture shall the soil receive,
> And every year increasing plenty give.
> Cleared from the woods more fruitful land they gain,
> And yellow Ceres fills the extended plain.
> Here bubbling fountains flow through every mede,
> Where flocks and herds delight to drink and feed.
> The marshy grounds improved rich meadows yield,
> The wilderness is made into a field."

---

[1] Colonial Records, IV., 312.